Continuing
Mandarin
Chinese
WORKBOOK

CORNELIUS C. KUBLER, Ph.D

T0160601

TUTTLE Publishing

Tokyo | Rutland, Vermont | Singapore

Published by Tuttle Publishing, an imprint of Periplus Editions (HK) Ltd.

www.tuttlepublishing.com

ISBN 978-0-8048-5139-8

Distributed by

North America, Latin America & Europe
Tuttle Publishing
364 Innovation Drive
North Clarendon,
VT 05759-9436 U.S.A.
Tel: 1 (802) 773-8930
Fax: 1 (802) 773-6993
info@tuttlepublishing.com
www.tuttlepublishing.com

Asia Pacific
Berkeley Books Pte. Ltd.
3 Kallang Sector #04-01
Singapore 349278
Tel: (65) 6741-2178
Fax: (65) 6741-2179
inquiries@periplus.com.sg
www.periplus.com

25 24 23 22 21 20

10 9 8 7 6 5 4 3 2 1

Printed in Singapore   2008TP

THE TUTTLE STORY
"Books to Span the East and West"

Our core mission at Tuttle Publishing is to create books which bring people together one page at a time. Tuttle was founded in 1832 in the small New England town of Rutland, Vermont (USA). Our fundamental values remain as strong today as they were then—to publish best-in-class books informing the English-speaking world about the countries and peoples of Asia. The world has become a smaller place today and Asia's economic, cultural and political influence has expanded, yet the need for meaningful dialogue and information about this diverse region has never been greater. Since 1948, Tuttle has been a leader in publishing books on the cultures, arts, cuisines, languages and literatures of Asia. Our authors and photographers have won numerous awards and Tuttle has published thousands of books on subjects ranging from martial arts to paper crafts. We welcome you to explore the wealth of information available on Asia at **www.tuttlepublishing.com**.

The Free Online Audio may be Downloaded.

How to Download the Free Online Audio of this Book.

1. You must have an internet connection.
2. Type the URL below into to your web browser.

    https://www.tuttlepublishing.com/continuing-mandarin-chinese-workbook

For support email us at info@tuttlepublishing.com.

Contents

Preface

This workbook is designed to accompany the textbook *Continuing Mandarin Chinese*. Used together, along with the audio files (available online for free), these materials will help learners raise their level in listening, speaking, reading, and writing Mandarin Chinese from the elementary to the intermediate level.

In a college or university environment, it is recommended that these materials be taught at the rate of approximately one lesson per week. Each lesson is divided into two parts, so Part One could be taken up on the first class day each week and Part Two on the second day, with the third day being used for review, testing, and supplemental activities. At this rate it would take 24 weeks to go through the materials. As most institutions schedule 25-35 weeks of instruction per academic year, this would still leave some time for other activities, or allow for a somewhat slower pace of going through the materials, if desired. The exact schedule and pace of progress will need to be determined based on local conditions.

The material in this workbook is meant to be done by students as homework outside of class, to strengthen and consolidate their language skills. Each lesson of the workbook contains two parts, each part including two listening comprehension exercises, one translation exercise, one character practice sheet, and one reading and writing exercise.

I wish to acknowledge here the following, who have been particularly helpful in the preparation and publication of these materials: Yang Wang, who created the drafts of the listening comprehension exercises; Jerling G. Kubler, who prepared the character practice sheets; Eric Oey; and Nancy Goh.

Cornelius C. Kubler
Department of Asian Studies, Williams College and
Institute for Advanced Studies, Shaanxi Normal University

LESSON 1
Getting Around Taipei

PART ONE

Listening Comprehension Exercises

NAME _____ COURSE _____ DATE _____

Based on the recorded passages, circle the best response to each of the questions that follow. You may listen to each passage as many times as needed.

EXERCISE ONE: QUESTIONS

1. **What is the woman doing right now?**

    (A) Buying things

    (B) Conversing with a Chinese student

    (C) Taking a taxi

2. **How long has the woman been learning Chinese?**

    (A) Five years

    (B) Six years

    (C) Seven years

3. **How long has the woman been in Beijing?**

    (A) One month

    (B) Two months

    (C) Three months

4. **What is the woman doing in Beijing?**

    (A) Studying at a college

    (B) Working at a bank

    (C) Working at an embassy

EXERCISE TWO: QUESTIONS

1. **Why is the one speaker hesitant about taking a taxi to the Summer Palace?**

    (A) It could be unsafe.

    (B) It would be expensive.

    (C) It might not be so convenient.

2. **Why is the other speaker hesitant about driving there themselves?**

    (A) It could be unsafe.

    (B) Parking might be a problem.

    (C) He isn't sure about how to get there.

3. **About how much does it cost to go to the Summer Palace by taxi?**

    (A) 50 RMB

    (B) 70 RMB

    (C) 90 RMB

4. **Where are the two speakers going to meet tomorrow?**

    (A) In the dorm

    (B) At the entrance to the school

    (C) At the front gate of the Summer Palace

Translation Exercise

NAME _____ COURSE _____ DATE _____

Translate the following sentences into Pinyin romanization with correct tone marks. If you have forgotten a word, consult the English-Chinese Glossary in the back of your textbook.

1. Relax, there is no problem.

2. Eat faster, we only have half an hour.

3. How long have you been in America?

4. That was terrifying! Drive more slowly, OK?

5. She has been working at the Bank of Taiwan for ten years.

Character Practice Sheet

NAME _____ COURSE _____ DATE _____

快	丶	忄	忄	忄	忙	快	快				
慢	丶	忄	忄	忄	忄	忄	忄	忄	慢	慢	
	慢	慢	慢	慢							
題	丨	冂	日	日	旦	早	早	是	是	是	
	是	是	題	題	題						
放	丶	亠	方	方	方	放	放	放			
解	丿	勹	夕	角	角	角	角	角	解	解	
	解	解	解								
決	丶	冫	冫	汩	決	決					

Reading and Writing Exercises

NAME _____   COURSE _____   DATE _____

A. **Transcribe what you hear in the online audio into Chinese characters.**

(1)

(2)

(3)

B. **If a reference is given after a question, answer based on the referenced part of the Reading Exercises. If no reference is indicated, you may answer any way you wish.**

(1) 王金金明天为什么要去机场？ B2

(2) 那个人觉得要决定的事，得怎么样？ C

(3) 你开车开得快不快？慢不慢？

(4) 你最近有没有什么问题需要解决？

PART TWO

Listening Comprehension Exercises

NAME _____ COURSE _____ DATE _____

Based on the recorded passages, circle the best response to each of the questions that follow. You may listen to each passage as many times as needed.

EXERCISE ONE: QUESTIONS

1. **Where does the woman want to go?**

    (A) Downtown

    (B) College campus

    (C) Zoo

2. **How much does it cost to go to Muzha?**

    (A) 20 NT

    (B) 25 NT

    (C) 30 NT

3. **How much did the female speaker spend on stored-value tickets?**

    (A) 300 NT

    (B) 500 NT

    (C) 600 NT

EXERCISE TWO: QUESTIONS

1. **In which city does this conversation take place?**

    (A) Beijing

    (B) Guangzhou

    (C) Shanghai

2. **How often does Bus 103 arrive?**

    (A) About every 5 minutes

    (B) About every 10 minutes

    (C) About every 15 minutes

3. **At which bus stop should the man get off?**

    (A) Huayuancun

    (B) Kejiguan

    (C) Nanmen

Translation Exercise

NAME _____   COURSE _____   DATE _____

Translate the following sentences into Pinyin romanization with correct tone marks. If you have forgotten a word, consult the English-Chinese Glossary in the back of your textbook.

1. **How often is there a bus?**

2. **There's a bus every fifteen minutes.**

3. **Strange, she hasn't come for two weeks.**

4. **I normally drive a car; I haven't taken the subway for a long time.**

5. **That's embarrassing; the $10 dollar ones are all sold out, only the $15 ones are left.**

Character Practice Sheet

NAME _____ COURSE _____ DATE _____

久	ノ	ク	久						
完	丶	ヽ	宀	宀	宀	宁	完		
或	一	丁	一	日	豆	或	或	或	
者	一	十	土	耂	耂	者	者	者	
再	一	丆	币	而	再	再			
见	丨	冂	贝	见					

Reading and Writing Exercises

NAME _____ COURSE _____ DATE _____

A. **Transcribe what you hear in the online audio into Chinese characters.**

(1)

(2)

(3)

B. **If a reference is given after a question, answer based on the referenced part of the Reading Exercises. If no reference is indicated, you may answer any way you wish.**

(1) 我们为什么可以回家了？ A7

(2) 这个人知道不知道他的外国朋友现在在哪里？ C1

(3) 请问，你去过香港或者台湾吗？

(4) 要是有一个人见到你和你说"好久不见!"，那么你应该说什么？

Asking Directions to a Friend's House

PART ONE

Listening Comprehension Exercises

NAME _____ COURSE _____ DATE _____

Based on the recorded passages, circle the best response to each of the questions that follow. You may listen to each passage as many times as needed.

EXERCISE ONE: QUESTIONS

1. **Where was the woman when this conversation took place?**

   (A) In an alley

   (B) At a bus station

   (C) Next to a bank

2. **In which direction is the speaker told to proceed?**

   (A) Toward the south

   (B) Toward the east

   (C) Toward the west

3. **How many more minutes will it take for the woman to reach her destination?**

   (A) About 3 minutes

   (B) About 5 minutes

   (C) About 8 minutes

EXERCISE TWO: QUESTIONS

1. **What is the basic problem?**

   (A) Someone is late.

   (B) The male speaker made a mistake.

   (C) The female speaker misread a map.

2. **Who is the guilty party?**

   (A) Little Zhang

   (B) The male speaker

   (C) The female speaker

3. **Besides the public restroom, what other landmark is mentioned?**

   (A) Bank

   (B) Post office

   (C) Store

4. **In the end, it turns out that after passing the public restroom, Little Zhang is supposed to go in what direction?**

   (A) Right

   (B) Left

   (C) Straight ahead

Translation Exercise

NAME _____ COURSE _____ DATE _____

Translate the following sentences into Pinyin romanization with correct tone marks. If you have forgotten a word, consult the English-Chinese Glossary in the back of your textbook.

1. Pay a little attention, don't miss it!

2. I tell you, their house is on the left, not on the right.

3. I'm first going to the post office; see you in a little while!

4. I'm very tired, but no matter how hard I try, I can't fall asleep.

5. I've been searching all over the place; no matter how hard I try, I can't find it.

Character Practice Sheet

NAME _____ COURSE _____ DATE _____

转	一	七	车	车	车	车	转	转		
跟	丨	口	口	무	무	무	足	趴	趴	趴
	跟	跟	跟							
讲	丶	讠	讠	讠	讲	讲				
具	丨	冂	月	月	目	且	具	具		
手	ノ	ニ	三	手						
房	丶	亠	亠	户	户	户	房	房		

Reading and Writing Exercises

NAME _____ COURSE _____ DATE _____

A. Transcribe what you hear in the online audio into Chinese characters.

(1)

(2)

(3)

B. If a reference is given after a question, answer based on the referenced part of the Reading Exercises. If no reference is indicated, you may answer any way you wish.

(1) 从这里去和平家具店，怎么走？ B2

(2) 那个人住的房子，左手边有什么，右手边有什么？ C

(3) 你住的房间里，家具多不多？

(4) 要是有人跟你讲中国话，你一定跟他讲中国话吗？

PART TWO

Listening Comprehension Exercises

NAME _____   COURSE _____   DATE _____

Based on the recorded passages, circle the best response to each of the questions that follow. You may listen to each passage as many times as needed.

EXERCISE ONE: QUESTIONS

1. **Starting when will the price of gasoline increase?**
    (A) Later today
    (B) Tomorrow
    (C) The day after tomorrow

2. **How much is 93-octane gasoline per liter?**
    (A) 4.65 RMB
    (B) 4.96 RMB
    (C) 4.97 RMB

3. **How many liters of gas does the man want?**
    (A) 20
    (B) 25
    (C) 30

EXERCISE TWO: QUESTIONS

1. **How much did the price of 93-octane gas increase per liter?**
    (A) 0.31RMB
    (B) 0.40 RMB
    (C) 0.41 RMB

2. **What kind of vehicle does the male speaker drive?**
    (A) Small car
    (B) Large car
    (C) Motorcycle

3. **Which kind of gasoline does the male speaker use?**
    (A) 93-octane gas
    (B) 95-octane gas
    (C) 97-octane gas

Translation Exercise

NAME _____ COURSE _____ DATE _____

Translate the following sentences into Pinyin romanization with correct tone marks. If you have forgotten a word, consult the English-Chinese Glossary in the back of your textbook.

1. I hear that Ms. Wang is coming again tomorrow.

2. The parking lot is close to here, a gas station is also not far away.

3. Beginning next month, the price of gas is going to be adjusted again.

4. This morning there are especially many cars that are filling up with gas.

5. Starting from last week, the weather has been getting hotter and hotter.

Character Practice Sheet

NAME _____ COURSE _____ DATE _____

加	フ	カ	加	加	加		
油	丶	氵	氵	氵| 汩	汩	油	油
满	丶	氵	氵	汀	汴	湔	洴	滞	满
	满	满	满				
特	ノ	一	牛	牛	牜	牜	牜	牜	特	特
价	ノ	亻	亻	价	价	价		
停	ノ	亻	亻	伫	伫	信	信	停	停
	停						

Reading and Writing Exercises

NAME _____ COURSE _____ DATE _____

A. Transcribe what you hear in the online audio into Chinese characters.

(1)

(2)

(3)

B. If a reference is given after a question, answer based on the referenced part of the Reading Exercises. If no reference is indicated, you may answer any way you wish.

(1) 那个人为什么说以后要坐公车或者走路去上班？C1

(2) 这两位大学校长要解决什么问题？C2

(3) 在美国，什么东西价钱特别贵？

(4) 你加油的时候，是不是一定加满？

Shopping

PART ONE

Listening Comprehension Exercises

NAME _____ COURSE _____ DATE _____

Based on the recorded passages, circle the best response to each of the questions that follow. You may listen to each passage as many times as needed.

EXERCISE ONE: QUESTIONS

1. **How much are backpacks?**
   (A) 65 RMB each
   (B) 70 RMB each
   (C) 130 RMB each

2. **In what color are backpacks NOT available?**
   (A) Black
   (B) Blue
   (C) Yellow

3. **How much money did the customer hand the salesman?**
   (A) 130 RMB
   (B) 150 RMB
   (C) 200 RMB

4. **With how many backpacks did the customer walk home?**
   (A) One
   (B) Two
   (C) Three

EXERCISE TWO: QUESTIONS

1. **What does the one speaker's daughter do?**
   (A) Have fun
   (B) Study
   (C) Work

2. **What does the other speaker's son do?**
   (A) Have fun
   (B) Study
   (C) Work

3. **Which college major is mentioned?**
   (A) Chinese
   (B) English
   (C) Japanese

Translation Exercise

NAME _____   COURSE _____   DATE _____

Translate the following sentences into Pinyin romanization with correct tone marks. If you have forgotten a word, consult the English-Chinese Glossary in the back of your textbook.

1.   **Now ice pops are two dollars each.**

2.   **Is her major Chinese or Japanese?**

3.   **Here's seven dollars in change; hold it carefully!**

4.   **Do you want to study in the English Department or the French Department?**

5.   **Little Li knows how to study but he doesn't know how to have fun.**

Character Practice Sheet

NAME ——————————————— COURSE ——————————— DATE ———————

根	一	十	才	木	朴	杚	杘	根	根	根
拿	ノ	人	入	人	合	合	合	含	拿	拿
专	一	二	专	专						
业	丨	丨丨	丨丨丨	业	业					
办	フ	力	办	办						
法	丶	丶丶	氵	汁	汁	注	法	法		

Reading and Writing Exercises

NAME_____ COURSE_____ DATE_____

A. Transcribe what you hear in the online audio into Chinese characters.

(1)

(2)

(3)

B. If a reference is given after a question, answer based on the referenced part of the Reading Exercises. If no reference is indicated, you may answer any way you wish.

(1) 那位女生的老师觉得加拿大的法文比较好听还是法国的法文比较好听？ B1

(2) 请问，那个人已经知道以后要找什么样的工作了吗？ C2

(3) 你已经决定你的专业了吗？

(4) 要是你找一个人可是他不在，你怎么办？

PART TWO

Listening Comprehension Exercises

NAME _____   COURSE _____   DATE _____

Based on the recorded passages, circle the best response to each of the questions that follow. You may listen to each passage as many times as needed.

EXERCISE ONE: QUESTIONS

1. **What did the customer want to buy?**

   (A) Ballpoint pens

   (B) Notebooks

   (C) Pencils

2. **How much does the customer have to pay in all?**

   (A) 6 RMB

   (B) 9.5 RMB

   (C) 12 RMB

3. **What color did the customer choose?**

   (A) Black

   (B) Blue

   (C) Red

EXERCISE TWO: QUESTIONS

1. **Where did the male speaker go?**

   (A) Bookstore

   (B) Newspaper kiosk

   (C) Post office

2. **Where did the female speaker go?**

   (A) Bookstore

   (B) Newspaper kiosk

   (C) Post office

3. **What did the male speaker buy?**

   (A) Dictionary

   (B) Newspaper

   (C) None of the above

4. **What did the female speaker buy?**

   (A) Dictionary

   (B) Magazine

   (C) None of the above

Translation Exercise

NAME _____   COURSE _____   DATE _____

Translate the following sentences into Pinyin romanization with correct tone marks. If you have forgotten a word, consult the English-Chinese Glossary in the back of your textbook.

1. Whose are those things?

2. Would you all like anything else?

3. I need an English-Chinese dictionary.

4. This kind of pencil is three dollars each.

5. I'd like to buy a newspaper, a notebook, and a map of Shanghai.

Character Practice Sheet

NAME _____ COURSE _____ DATE _____

想	一	十	才	木	机	机	相	相	相
	想	想	想						相
种	丿	二	千	千	禾	利	和	和	种
书	乛	乛	书	书					
些	丨	卜	止	止	止	此	些	些	
报	一	十	扌	扌	护	抈	报		
纸	乚	纟	纟	纟	纤	纸	纸		

Reading and Writing Exercises

NAME _____ COURSE _____ DATE _____

A. **Transcribe what you hear in the online audio into Chinese characters.**

(1)

(2)

(3)

B. **If a reference is given after a question, answer based on the referenced part of the Reading Exercises. If no reference is indicated, you may answer any way you wish.**

(1) 哪种本子好像有两百张纸？是这种还是那种？A9

(2) 那个人现在很想到哪儿去买什么？C2

(3) 你正在想什么呢？

(4) 你喜欢看报纸吗？你看什么报纸？

Buying Vegetables and Fruits

PART ONE

Listening Comprehension Exercises

NAME _____ COURSE _____ DATE _____

Based on the recorded passages, circle the best response to each of the questions that follow. You may listen to each passage as many times as needed.

EXERCISE ONE: QUESTIONS

1. **What is true about the celery?**

   (A) It's crisp and looks nice.

   (B) It costs 5.70 per catty.

   (C) It's imported from Japan.

2. **Name one item the woman bought yesterday.**

   (A) Cabbage

   (B) Celery

   (C) Tomatoes

3. **How much is the cabbage per catty?**

   (A) 2 RMB

   (B) 3 RMB

   (C) 7.50 RMB

4. **What is the total price the woman will pay for the cabbage?**

   (A) 2 RMB

   (B) 4 RMB

   (C) 6 RMB

EXERCISE TWO: QUESTIONS

1. **Which phrase would best describe the man?**

   (A) He's a good father.

   (B) He's slightly annoyed.

   (C) He knows how to bargain.

2. **What did the woman buy?**

   (A) Celery

   (B) Lettuce

   (C) Tomatoes

3. **When did this conversation take place?**

   (A) 1:30 PM

   (B) 2:10 PM

   (C) 2:30 PM

4. **What is the woman supposed to do in a little while?**

   (A) Buy groceries

   (B) Call her child

   (C) Wait for the man

Translation Exercise

NAME _____   COURSE _____   DATE _____

Translate the following sentences into Pinyin romanization with correct tone marks. If you have forgotten a word, consult the English-Chinese Glossary in the back of your textbook.

1. I only just arrived this morning.

2. Their celery is both fresh and crisp.

3. How come vegetables are so expensive?

4. A: How much is cabbage? B: 20 dollars per catty.

5. These green vegetables were all imported from abroad

Character Practice Sheet

NAME _____ COURSE _____ DATE _____

才	一	十	才						
斤	丿	厂	斤	斤					
菜	一	十	艹	艹	芏	芸	苹	苹	菜
	菜								
白	丿	亻	门	白	白				
保	丿	亻	亻	伫	伫	伢	伢	保	
证	丶	讠	证	证	证	证	证		

Reading and Writing Exercises

NAME _____ COURSE _____ DATE _____

A. **Transcribe what you hear in the online audio into Chinese characters.**

(1)

(2)

(3)

B. **If a reference is given after a question, answer based on the referenced part of the Reading Exercises. If no reference is indicated, you may answer any way you wish.**

(1) 到了加拿大之后，"我"才知道什么？ A5

(2) 要是买一斤白菜，要多少钱？ B1

(3) 你能保证这个菜好吃吗？

(4) 你喜欢不喜欢吃中国菜？

PART TWO

Listening Comprehension Exercises

NAME _____   COURSE _____   DATE _____

Based on the recorded passages, circle the best response to each of the questions that follow. You may listen to each passage as many times as needed.

EXERCISE ONE: QUESTIONS

1. **What do the two speakers decide to buy?**
   (A) Bananas
   (B) Grapes
   (C) Pears

2. **According to the passage, how do bananas and grapes compare?**
   (A) Bananas are cheaper than grapes.
   (B) Grapes are fresher than bananas.
   (C) The passage provides no information about this.

3. **According to the passage, how do bananas and pears compare?**
   (A) Bananas are cheaper than pears.
   (B) Pears are fresher than bananas.
   (C) The passage provides no information about this.

EXERCISE TWO: QUESTIONS

1. **What kind of fruit did the woman look at first?**
   (A) Apples
   (B) Peaches
   (C) Pears

2. **How much were they per catty?**
   (A) 2 RMB per catty
   (B) 2.5 RMB per catty
   (C) 4.5 RMB per catty

3. **What kind of fruit did the woman look at later?**
   (A) Apples
   (B) Peaches
   (C) Pears

4. **How much did she pay for the second kind of fruit she looked at?**
   (A) 2 RMB per catty
   (B) 2.5 RMB per catty
   (C) 4.5 RMB per catty

Translation Exercise

NAME _____ COURSE _____ DATE _____

Translate the following sentences into Pinyin romanization with correct tone marks. If you have forgotten a word, consult the English-Chinese Glossary in the back of your textbook.

1. The fruit here is much prettier than the fruit there.

2. I'll give you $6.50 in change; please count your change!

3. The apples and the oranges, please wrap them up for me.

4. This kind of grape tastes much better than that kind of grape.

5. Please weigh me out three catties of peaches; pick out fresher ones.

Character Practice Sheet

NAME _____ COURSE _____ DATE _____

总	丶	丷	丷	丷	乴	乴	总	总	总
包	丿	勹	勺	匂	包				
水	亅	丿	才	水					
果	丨	冂	曰	日	旦	甲	果	果	
语	丶	讠	讠	订	评	评	语	语	
言	丶	亠	言	言	言	言	言		

Reading and Writing Exercises

NAME _____ COURSE _____ DATE _____

A. **Transcribe what you hear in the online audio into Chinese characters.**

(1)

(2)

(3)

B. **If a reference is given after a question, answer based on the referenced part of the Reading Exercises. If no reference is indicated, you may answer any way you wish.**

(1) 手里拿着公事包的那位老师叫什么名字？ A3

(2) 那个人以后要是有钱，想吃进口的菜和进口的什么东西？ C1

(3) 你总共会说几种语言？

(4) 你有没有公事包？你的中文老师呢？

At the Market

PART ONE

Listening Comprehension Exercises

NAME _____ COURSE _____ DATE _____

Based on the recorded passages, circle the best response to each of the questions that follow. You may listen to each passage as many times as needed.

EXERCISE ONE: QUESTIONS

1. **What is the price of the apples the woman decided to buy?**
   (A) 2.5 RMB per catty
   (B) 4 RMB per catty
   (C) 10 RMB per catty

2. **What else did the female speaker want to buy?**
   (A) Bananas
   (B) Beef
   (C) Bread

3. **In what direction should the female speaker go in order to get to the grocery store?**
   (A) Turn right
   (B) Turn left
   (C) Go straight

EXERCISE TWO: QUESTIONS

1. **What does one of the speakers claim?**
   (A) In China men eat meat.
   (B) In China there are many vegetarians.
   (C) In China many women are vegetarians.

2. **What kind of meat is favored by the people from north China?**
   (A) Mutton
   (B) Chicken
   (C) Duck

3. **What can be inferred from the conversation?**
   (A) One of the speakers seldom eats meat.
   (B) One of the speakers doesn't eat poultry.
   (C) One of the speakers is from north China.

Translation Exercise

NAME _____   COURSE _____   DATE _____

Translate the following sentences into Pinyin romanization with correct tone marks. If you have forgotten a word, consult the English-Chinese Glossary in the back of your textbook.

1. This meat is not the least bit fat.

2. Is there a bakery in the vicinity?

3. The grocery store is extremely close.

4. She doesn't eat fish or shrimp; she's a vegetarian.

5. Please weigh me out ¥ 10.00 worth of chicken meat.

Character Practice Sheet

NAME _____ COURSE _____ DATE _____

切	一	七	切	切				
肉	丨	冂	内	内	肉	肉		
牛	丿	𠂉	𠂔	牛				
极	一	十	才	木	杉	极	极	
食	丿	𠆢	仐	今	仐	仝	食	食	食
品	丨	冂	口	吕	吊	品	品	品

Reading and Writing Exercises

NAME _____ COURSE _____ DATE _____

A. **Transcribe what you hear in the online audio into Chinese characters.**

(1)

(2)

(3)

B. **If a reference is given after a question, answer based on the referenced part of the Reading Exercises. If no reference is indicated, you may answer any way you wish.**

(1) 小李现在的这个工作忙不忙？ C1

(2) 为什么那个人切肉、切菜的时候，他小妹离他很远？ C2

(3) 美国的食品店卖什么？

(4) 你比较喜欢吃面包跟牛肉，还是面包跟水果？

PART TWO

Listening Comprehension Exercises

NAME _____ COURSE _____ DATE _____

Based on the recorded passages, circle the best response to each of the questions that follow. You may listen to each passage as many times as needed.

EXERCISE ONE: QUESTIONS

1. **Is there a Costco in Taipei?**

    (A) No, there isn't.

    (B) Yes, there is one.

    (C) Yes, there are several.

2. **What does the male speaker want to buy at Costco?**

    (A) Beef

    (B) Bread

    (C) Vegetables

3. **What does the female speaker want to buy at Costco?**

    (A) Beef

    (B) Bread

    (C) Vegetables

4. **When will the two speakers meet again?**

    (A) In about 15 minutes

    (B) In about 30 minutes

    (C) In about an hour

EXERCISE TWO: QUESTIONS

1. **At what age did the male speaker learn how to drive?**

    (A) 16

    (B) 17

    (C) 18

2. **According to the passage, how does the younger generation in China differ from the older generation?**

    (A) They're better educated.

    (B) They're more willing to spend money.

    (C) They're more influenced by Western culture.

3. **Which of the following statements is NOT true?**

    (A) Nowadays there are many cars in Beijing.

    (B) American cars are bigger than Chinese cars.

    (C) There are more buses in the U.S. than in China.

Translation Exercise

NAME _____ COURSE _____ DATE _____

Translate the following sentences into Pinyin romanization with correct tone marks. If you have forgotten a word, consult the English-Chinese Glossary in the back of your textbook.

1. I feel that Chinese is easier day by day.

2. She bought beef, mutton, fish, shrimp and so on.

3. China's bakeries are not as common as France's.

4. In order to save money, we decided not to eat lunch.

5. What are Shanghai's supermarkets like compared to America's?

Character Practice Sheet

NAME _____ COURSE _____ DATE _____

土	一 十 土
节	一 十 艹 节 节
入	丿 入
主	、 亠 主 丯 主
意	、 亠 产 立 产 音 音 音 音 意 意 意
思	丨 冂 冋 甲 田 田 思 思 思

Reading and Writing Exercises

NAME _____   COURSE _____   DATE _____

A. **Transcribe what you hear in the online audio into Chinese characters.**

(1)

(2)

(3)

B. **If a reference is given after a question, answer based on the referenced part of the Reading Exercises. If no reference is indicated, you may answer any way you wish.**

(1) 入口在哪儿？ 出口在哪儿？ A3

(2) 那个人的弟弟、妹妹主张什么？ A5

(3) 你很节省吗？

(4) 中文学起来很有意思吧？

Purchasing Shoes and Clothing

PART ONE

Listening Comprehension Exercises

NAME _____ COURSE _____ DATE _____

Based on the recorded passages, circle the best response to each of the questions that follow. You may listen to each passage as many times as needed.

EXERCISE ONE: QUESTIONS

1. **What should the shoes the customer wants be like?**

   (A) They should be grey in color.

   (B) They should be high-heeled shoes.

   (C) They should be made of leather.

2. **What is the customer's Chinese shoe size?**

   (A) 7

   (B) 36

   (C) 37

3. **How much is the pair of shoes she looks at?**

   (A) 920 RMB

   (B) 1200 RMB

   (C) 2100 RMB

4. **In the end, why doesn't the customer buy the shoes?**

   (A) They don't fit right.

   (B) They're priced too high.

   (C) They're imported from America.

EXERCISE TWO: QUESTIONS

1. **About how long has Professor Li been in the U.S.?**

   (A) About five months

   (B) About ten months

   (C) About a year

2. **What does Professor Li like about the U.S.?**

   (A) America is clean.

   (B) America has many cars.

   (C) Transportation in America is convenient.

3. **What about the U.S. does Professor Li not like so much?**

   (A) Crime is rather high.

   (B) America has too many cars.

   (C) America has few buses.

Translation Exercise

NAME _____   COURSE _____   DATE _____

Translate the following sentences into Pinyin romanization with correct tone marks. If you have forgotten a word, consult the English-Chinese Glossary in the back of your textbook.

1. I wear size 32; what size do you wear?

2. This kind and that kind are completely different.

3. I'm a student; could you reduce the price a little?

4. This pair of socks is one size bigger; that pair is one size smaller.

5. This pair of shoes is pretty, all right, but ¥ 400.00 is too expensive.

Character Practice Sheet

NAME _____ COURSE _____ DATE _____

双	フ	又	双	双					
鞋	一	十	廿	廿	艹	芦	苎	苜	革	革
	革	革	鞋	鞋	鞋				
黑	丨	冂	冂	冈	四	甲	里	里	黑
	黑	黑							
色	丿	⺈	占	召	色	色			
穿	丶	八	宀	宀	穴	空	空	穷	穿
算	丿	⺮	⺮	⺮	⺮	竹	竹	管	管	管
	笪	笪	算	算					

Reading and Writing Exercises

NAME_____ COURSE_____ DATE_____

A. **Transcribe what you hear in the online audio into Chinese characters.**

(1)

(2)

(3)

B. **If a reference is given after a question, answer based on the referenced part of the Reading Exercises. If no reference is indicated, you may answer any way you wish.**

(1) 那双黑鞋为什么价钱这么贵？ A3

(2) 她们为什么决定一个人买黑色的高跟鞋，一个人买白色的高跟鞋？ C1

(3) 你穿几号的鞋？

(4) 你在你现在住的地方总共有几双鞋？

PART TWO

Listening Comprehension Exercises

NAME _____ COURSE _____ DATE _____

Based on the recorded passages, circle the best response to each of the questions that follow. You may listen to each passage as many times as needed.

EXERCISE ONE: QUESTIONS

1. **For whom is the skirt?**

   (A) For the female speaker

   (B) For the female speaker's daughter

   (C) For someone else

2. **How much of a discount is she offered?**

   (A) 30% off

   (B) 50% off

   (C) 70% off

3. **In the end, does the woman purchase the skirt?**

   (A) Yes, she pays for it with cash.

   (B) Yes, she pays for it with a credit card.

   (C) No, she doesn't, because it's too short.

EXERCISE TWO: QUESTIONS

1. **What did the male speaker buy?**

   (A) A shirt

   (B) A pair of pants

   (C) A pair of shoes

2. **What color did he end up deciding on?**

   (A) Black

   (B) Blue

   (C) Green

3. **What was the male speaker most concerned about?**

   (A) Whether there was a discount on the price

   (B) Whether his brother would like the color

   (C) Whether he could use a credit card for the purchase

4. **Does the store accept returns for exchange?**

   (A) Within one week

   (B) Within two weeks

   (C) Within a month

Translation Exercise

NAME _____   COURSE _____   DATE _____

Translate the following sentences into Pinyin romanization with correct tone marks. If you have forgotten a word, consult the English-Chinese Glossary in the back of your textbook.

1. If I have time, I'll definitely go.

2. Please come over and take a look.

3. It can be exchanged within 30 days.

4. This kind of pants today just happens to be 20% off.

5. A: Can one use a credit card here? B: Sorry, we don't accept credit cards.

Character Practice Sheet

NAME _____ COURSE _____ DATE _____

应	、	一	广	广	应	应	应		
该	、	讠	讠	讠	该	该	该	该	
衣	、	一	广	衣	衣	衣			
服	丿	刀	月	月	刖	刖	服	服	
如	乂	女	女	如	如	如			
内	丨	冂	内	内					

Reading and Writing Exercises

NAME _____ COURSE _____ DATE _____

A. **Transcribe what you hear in the online audio into Chinese characters.**

(1)

(2)

(3)

B. **If a reference is given after a question, answer based on the referenced part of the Reading Exercises. If no reference is indicated, you may answer any way you wish.**

(1) 年家平说他什么时候给李老师他的作业？ B2

(2) 那个人保证下次如果还去广州的话，一定会多带一些什么？为什么？ C1

(3) 雨衣应该什么时候穿？

(4) 你如果需要买衣服的话，到哪儿去买？

Ordering a Meal in a Restaurant

PART ONE

Listening Comprehension Exercises

NAME _____ COURSE _____ DATE _____

Based on the recorded passages, circle the best response to each of the questions that follow. You may listen to each passage as many times as needed.

EXERCISE ONE: QUESTIONS

1. **Which meal of the day are the two speakers about to have?**
   (A) Breakfast
   (B) Lunch
   (C) Dinner

2. **What kind of restaurant does the man want to go to?**
   (A) Sichuan
   (B) Vegetarian
   (C) It doesn't matter.

3. **What kind of meat does the female speaker prefer?**
   (A) Chicken
   (B) Mutton
   (C) Pork

4. **How many dishes do they order?**
   (A) Two
   (B) Three
   (C) Four

EXERCISE TWO: QUESTIONS

1. **Not including the soup, how many dishes are the two speakers having?**
   (A) Two
   (B) Three
   (C) Four

2. **How many bowls of rice did they order in all?**
   (A) One
   (B) Two
   (C) Three

3. **Where is the restroom?**
   (A) At the end of the hallway
   (B) On the right-hand side of the hallway
   (C) On the left-hand side of the hallway

Translation Exercise

NAME _____   COURSE _____   DATE _____

Translate the following sentences into Pinyin romanization with correct tone marks. If you have forgotten a word, consult the English-Chinese Glossary in the back of your textbook.

1.   **Is ten dollars enough?**

2.   **As you wish; any day will do.**

3.   **Anything is fine; why don't you decide.**

4.   **That child doesn't yet know how to eat with chopsticks.**

5.   **One order of Pockmarked Old Woman's Tofu. And also bring a bowl of egg soup.**

Character Practice Sheet

NAME _____ COURSE _____ DATE _____

随	了	阝	阝¯	阝ㄅ	阝ㅑ	防	陏	陏	陏	随
	随									
便	ノ	亻	仁	仁	仃	仴	佰	便	便	
用	ノ	几	月	月	用					
够	ノ	ク	勹	句	句	句ʹ	够	够	够	
	够									
爸	ノ	八	父	父	爷	爷	爷	爸		
妈	く	女	女	女刀	妈	妈				

Reading and Writing Exercises

NAME _____ COURSE _____ DATE _____

A. Transcribe what you hear in the online audio into Chinese characters.

(1)

(2)

(3)

B. **If a reference is given after a question, answer based on the referenced part of the Reading Exercises. If no reference is indicated, you may answer any way you wish.**

(1) 王大海是用左手写字还是用右手写字？你觉得这是为什么？ A10

(2) 那个美国人想在哪儿吃饭？ B1

(3) 五百块够不够你用一个月？

(4) 你爸爸妈妈会不会说中国话？

PART TWO

Listening Comprehension Exercises

NAME _____   COURSE _____   DATE _____

Based on the recorded passages, circle the best response to each of the questions that follow. You may listen to each passage as many times as needed.

EXERCISE ONE: QUESTIONS

1. **What will the two men order as their staple food?**

   (A) Dumplings

   (B) Rice

   (C) Steamed buns

2. **What kind of foods can Li Tong not eat?**

   (A) Hot spicy foods

   (B) Salty foods

   (C) Foods containing meat

3. **Which of the following foods was NOT ordered?**

   (A) Tofu

   (B) Pork

   (C) Green vegetables

EXERCISE TWO: QUESTIONS

1. **Where is the male speaker from?**

   (A) Mainland China

   (B) Taiwan

   (C) Overseas

2. **Where is the foreigner who is mentioned from?**

   (A) England

   (B) Japan

   (C) U.S.

3. **The man requests that the food not be too what?**

   (A) Hot spicy

   (B) Salty

   (C) Sweet

4. **How many bottles of beer does the man order for himself and his friend?**

   (A) One

   (B) Two

   (C) Three

Translation Exercise

Translate the following sentences into Pinyin romanization with correct tone marks. If you have forgotten a word, consult the English-Chinese Glossary in the back of your textbook.

1. **Eat more, drink more!**

2. **I have an urgent matter; please hurry up.**

3. **The books, now you can put them on the table.**

4. **Please don't put in too much meat.** (="Please put in less meat.")

5. **In Hong Kong, only when you've reached the age of 18 can you buy alcohol.**

Character Practice Sheet

NAME _____ COURSE _____ DATE _____

受	´	⺆	⺆	⺤	⺤	乑	受	受		
米	`	⺀	⺓	半	米	米				
系	⺀	⺀	乏	玄	予	糸	系			
急	⺈	⺈	刍	刍	刍	刍	急	急	急	
喝	Ｉ	�口	口	口´	叩	叩	叩	叩	喝	喝
	喝	喝								
酒	`	⺀	氵	汀	沂	沔	洒	酒	酒	

Reading and Writing Exercises

NAME _____ COURSE _____ DATE _____

A. Transcribe what you hear in the online audio into Chinese characters.

(1)

(2)

(3)

B. If a reference is given after a question, answer based on the referenced part of the Reading Exercises. If no reference is indicated, you may answer any way you wish.

(1) 你觉得，金小姐跟李先生大概是什么关系？A8

(2) 小李为什么不能吃了饭再走？B1

(3) 您喜欢喝酒吗？

(4) 你如果有一天没有米饭吃，你受得了吗？

Arranging a Banquet

PART ONE

Listening Comprehension Exercises

NAME _____ COURSE _____ DATE _____

Based on the recorded passages, circle the best response to each of the questions that follow. You may listen to each passage as many times as needed.

EXERCISE ONE: QUESTIONS

1. **On which date will the banquet be held?**

    (A) The 25th

    (B) The 27th

    (C) The 28th

2. **How many people will attend the banquet?**

    (A) About 50

    (B) About 80

    (C) About 100

3. **What price level did the male speaker book?**

    (A) 80 RMB per person

    (B) 100 RMB per person

    (C) 150 RMB per person

EXERCISE TWO: QUESTIONS

1. **For what time is the dinner reservation?**

    (A) 5:30 PM

    (B) 6:30 PM

    (C) 7:30 PM

2. **What type of cuisine will be served?**

    (A) Chinese

    (B) Japanese

    (C) Western

3. **About how many persons will be attending?**

    (A) Six people

    (B) Eight people

    (C) Ten people

Translation Exercise

NAME _____   COURSE _____   DATE _____

Translate the following sentences into Pinyin romanization with correct tone marks. If you have forgotten a word, consult the English-Chinese Glossary in the back of your textbook.

1. **What price level do you all plan to book?**

2. **I don't know how to cook; can you teach me?**

3. **I think dividing into three tables would be good.**

4. **I reckon there will be about 50 people participating.**

5. **Do you prefer** ("relatively like to eat") **Chinese-style food or Western-style food?**

Character Practice Sheet

NAME _____ COURSE _____ DATE _____

桌	丿	⺊	⼧	占	占	卣	卓	桌	桌
席	丶	亠	广	广	庐	庐	庐	庐	席
参	㇒	ㅿ	厶	纟	矣	参	参	参	
每	丿	𠂉	亡	母	每	每	每		
元	一	二	亓	元					
做	丿	亻	仁	什	什	估	估	做	做
做									

Reading and Writing Exercises

NAME _____ COURSE _____ DATE _____

A. Transcribe what you hear in the online audio into Chinese characters.

(1)

(2)

(3)

B. If a reference is given after a question, answer based on the referenced part of the Reading Exercises. If no reference is indicated, you may answer any way you wish.

(1) 毛主席是哪年在哪儿出生的？ A9

(2) 张小姐明天打不打算参加那个酒席？席先生呢？ B2

(3) 你每天都做些什么？

(4) 你以后要不要做买卖？

PART TWO

Listening Comprehension Exercises

NAME _____   COURSE _____   DATE _____

Based on the recorded passages, circle the best response to each of the questions that follow. You may listen to each passage as many times as needed.

EXERCISE ONE: QUESTIONS

1. **Who is going to arrange the menu?**

    (A) Mr. Li

    (B) Mr. Li's secretary

    (C) The restaurant

2. **How many warm dishes will there be at the dinner?**

    (A) Two

    (B) Six

    (C) Eight

3. **What else will there be at the dinner?**

    (A) Cold dishes

    (B) Spicy hot dishes

    (C) Fruit

4. **What will be the overall flavor of the dishes?**

    (A) Salty

    (B) Spicy

    (C) Sweet

EXERCISE TWO: QUESTIONS

1. **Where does this conversation occur?**

    (A) In an office

    (B) On the telephone

    (C) In a person's home

2. **What is the surname of the person being sought?**

    (A) Zhān

    (B) Zhāng

    (C) Zhuāng

3. **When will this person be back?**

    (A) Around 2:30 PM

    (B) Around 3:00 PM

    (C) Around 4:00 PM

4. **What does the woman want?**

    (A) To ask questions

    (B) To sell products

    (C) To visit her old classmate

Translation Exercise

NAME _____   COURSE _____   DATE _____

Translate the following sentences into Pinyin romanization with correct tone marks. If you have forgotten a word, consult the English-Chinese Glossary in the back of your textbook.

1. (We) welcome you to contact us.

2. We're not very familiar with your Taiwanese cuisine.

3. I myself know how to do it; you don't need to help me.

4. Please leave your phone number so we can contact you.

5. The dishes, is it that you yourselves will order them, or that they are arranged by us?

Character Practice Sheet

NAME _____ COURSE _____ DATE _____

自	´	⺆	⺆	自	自	自			
己	⺆	コ	己						
风	ノ	几	凡	风					
味	l	⼝	⼝	⼝	咊	咊	味	味	
由	l	⼝	冃	由	由				
留	´	⺈	⼙	幻	幼	留	留	留	留

Reading and Writing Exercises

NAME _____ COURSE _____ DATE _____

A. **Transcribe what you hear in the online audio into Chinese characters.**

(1)

(2)

(3)

B. **If a reference is given after a question, answer based on the referenced part of the Reading Exercises. If no reference is indicated, you may answer any way you wish.**

(1) 这个问题得由谁决定？A4

(2) 何小山为什么自己一个人到加拿大留学去了？A8

(3) 你比较喜欢吃什么风味的菜？

(4) 你想不想到北京或者台北去留学？

Peking Duck

PART ONE

Listening Comprehension Exercises

NAME _____ COURSE _____ DATE _____

Based on the recorded passages, circle the best response to each of the questions that follow. You may listen to each passage as many times as needed.

EXERCISE ONE: QUESTIONS

1. **How long has the man been learning English?**

    (A) Two months

    (B) Two years

    (C) Five and one-half years

2. **How long has the woman been in China?**

    (A) Two months

    (B) Two years

    (C) Five and one-half years

3. **Why is the woman at first hesitant about speaking?**

    (A) She doesn't like to speak in public.

    (B) She lacks confidence in her Chinese.

    (C) She doesn't know what she should say.

4. **What was the main reason for this occasion?**

    (A) It was the woman's birthday.

    (B) The woman wanted to express her appreciation.

    (C) The man and the woman wanted to discuss language learning.

EXERCISE TWO: QUESTIONS

1. **How many times has Professor He been to China before?**

    (A) One time

    (B) Two times

    (C) Three times

2. **How long does Professor He plan to stay this time?**

    (A) Two months

    (B) Three months

    (C) Four months

3. **How long has Professor He been here already?**

    (A) Two months

    (B) Three months

    (C) Four months

4. **Where does this conversation most likely take place?**

    (A) Classroom

    (B) Office

    (C) Restaurant

Translation Exercise

NAME _____   COURSE _____   DATE _____

Translate the following sentences into Pinyin romanization with correct tone marks. If you have forgotten a word, consult the English-Chinese Glossary in the back of your textbook.

1. All right, I'll simply say a few phrases.

2. Now I and my husband will toast you all.

3. Welcome everybody to come here to get together for a meal.

4. I wish you that your work goes smoothly and that your life is happy.

5. I very much thank everyone for the help and care you've given us these past few months.

Character Practice Sheet

NAME _____ COURSE _____ DATE _____

非	丨	亅	刲	刲	刲	非	非	非		
常	丶	丷	丷	丷	丷	屵	常	岢	营	常
	常									
简	丿	𠂉	𠂆	竹	竹	竹	竹	竹	简	简
	简	简	简							
单	丶	丷	丷	丷	屵	单	単	单		
句	丿	勹	勹	句	句					
活	丶	冫	氵	氵	沪	汗	汗	活	活	

Reading and Writing Exercises

NAME _____ COURSE _____ DATE _____

A. Transcribe what you hear in the online audio into Chinese characters.

(1)

(2)

(3)

B. If a reference is given after a question, answer based on the referenced part of the Reading Exercises. If no reference is indicated, you may answer any way you wish.

(1) 那位同学中文怎么样？日文怎么样？A3

(2) 小王常常会晚一点儿到，她的上司有没有说什么？A3

(3) 你平常早上几点钟起床？

(4) 你喜欢过简单的生活吗？

PART TWO

Listening Comprehension Exercises

NAME _____ COURSE _____ DATE _____

Based on the recorded passages, circle the best response to each of the questions that follow. You may listen to each passage as many times as needed.

EXERCISE ONE: QUESTIONS

1. **What is the Chinese man's surname?**
   (A) Zhāng
   (B) Zhōng
   (C) Zhèng

2. **What kind of meat are they eating?**
   (A) Duck
   (B) Mutton
   (C) Pork

3. **Where did Mr. Smith have this dish before?**
   (A) Beijing
   (B) New York City
   (C) Shanghai

4. **How many glasses of alcohol has Mr. Smith already had?**
   (A) One
   (B) Four
   (C) Seven

EXERCISE TWO: QUESTIONS

1. **How many bottles of beer has the male speaker drunk?**
   (A) Four
   (B) Five
   (C) Six

2. **How would the emotions of the female speaker be best described?**
   (A) Happy
   (B) Sad
   (C) Angry

Translation Exercise

NAME _____   COURSE _____   DATE _____

Translate the following sentences into Pinyin romanization with correct tone marks.

Translate the following sentences into Pinyin romanization with correct tone marks. If you have forgotten a word, consult the English-Chinese Glossary in the back of your textbook.

1. A: Taste this dish! B: Thank you, I'll help myself.

2. The host is not drunk, but the guests are all drunk.

3. The roast duck, the more you eat it, the better it tastes.

4. This dish, I heard of it long ago, but I've never ever eaten it before.

5. Have you ever eaten Ants Climb Trees before? (use **-guo...méiyou**)

Character Practice Sheet

NAME _____ COURSE _____ DATE _____

各	ノ	ク	久	各	各	各		
客	丶	宀	宀	宀	夕	宏	客	客
习	フ	习	习					
惯	丶	八	忄	忙	忙	忙	怖	惯	惯
惯								
认	丶	讠	认	认				
识	丶	讠	识	识	识	识		

Reading and Writing Exercises

NAME _____ COURSE _____ DATE _____

A. Transcribe what you hear in the online audio into Chinese characters.

(1)

(2)

(3)

B. If a reference is given after a question, answer based on the referenced part of the Reading Exercises. If no reference is indicated, you may answer any way you wish.

(1) 各国的生活习惯都一样吗？ A1

(2) 如果法国人家里有客人，他们会怎么样？ A8

(3) 你认识多少个中国字？

(4) 你每天学习几个钟头？

More Peking Duck and Making Dumplings

PART ONE

Listening Comprehension Exercises

NAME _____ COURSE _____ DATE _____

Based on the recorded passages, circle the best response to each of the questions that follow. You may listen to each passage as many times as needed.

EXERCISE ONE: QUESTIONS

1. **What time is it now?**
   (A) 9:00 AM
   (B) 10:30 AM
   (C) 4:30 PM

2. **What will the speakers do first?**
   (A) Have lunch
   (B) Have dinner
   (C) Go to the Summer Palace

3. **What season is it in Beijing right now?**
   (A) Spring
   (B) Summer
   (C) Winter

4. **What problem does the woman see regarding the article of clothing that is mentioned?**
   (A) Too thin
   (B) Too heavy
   (C) Too thick

EXERCISE TWO: QUESTIONS

1. **How many people are eating?**
   (A) Two
   (B) Three
   (C) Four

2. **How many dishes has the male speaker already ordered?**
   (A) Four
   (B) Five
   (C) Six

3. **What else is the male speaker going to order?**
   (A) A soup
   (B) A vegetable dish
   (C) A dessert

Translation Exercise

NAME _____   COURSE _____   DATE _____

Translate the following sentences into Pinyin romanization with correct tone marks. If you have forgotten a word, consult the English-Chinese Glossary in the back of your textbook.

1. **Take the pancake and roll it up.**

2. **Put the paper and pens on the table.**

3. **Chinese people first eat food and then drink soup.**

4. **First take a pancake and then put on scallions.**

5. **We've eaten too much; we really can't eat any more.**

Character Practice Sheet

NAME ——————————————— COURSE ——————————— DATE ———————

把	一	十	扌	扩	扣	扣	把			
夫	一	二	夫	夫						
感	一	厂	厂	厈	厈	咸	咸	咸	咸	咸`
	感	感	感							
及	丿	乃	及							
更	一	丆	丙	両	百	更	更			
笑	丿	⼂	⺮	⺮	竹	竹	竺	竺	竿	笑

Reading and Writing Exercises

NAME _____ COURSE _____ DATE _____

A. Transcribe what you hear in the online audio into Chinese characters.

(1)

(2)

(3)

B. If a reference is given after a question, answer based on the referenced part of the Reading Exercises. If no reference is indicated, you may answer any way you wish.

(1) 中国北方人习惯吃面，南方人更喜欢吃什么？你呢？ A2

(2) 他们现在生活过得那么好，应该感谢谁？ A4

(3) 你是一个喜欢讲笑话的人吗？

(4) 你常常把鞋子放在桌子上吗？

PART TWO

Listening Comprehension Exercises

NAME _____ COURSE _____ DATE _____

Based on the recorded passages, circle the best response to each of the questions that follow. You may listen to each passage as many times as needed.

EXERCISE ONE: QUESTIONS

1. **How busy is Miss Li?**

    (A) She is not as busy as Mr. He.

    (B) She is as busy as Mr. He.

    (C) She is busier than Mr. He.

2. **Why has Mr. He been busy recently?**

    (A) He has a lot of homework.

    (B) He has to take care of his child.

    (C) He has especially much work at the office.

3. **How old is Mr. He's child?**

    (A) One and a half years old

    (B) Two years old

    (C) Two and a half years old

EXERCISE TWO: QUESTIONS

1. **How many dumplings will the woman boil for the man?**

    (A) 12

    (B) 16

    (C) 20

2. **When will the dumplings be served?**

    (A) At lunch

    (B) At dinner

    (C) Right away

3. **Which item below is NOT in the dumpling filling?**

    (A) Beef

    (B) Cabbage

    (C) Eggs

Translation Exercise

NAME _____   COURSE _____   DATE _____

Translate the following sentences into Pinyin romanization with correct tone marks. If you have forgotten a word, consult the English-Chinese Glossary in the back of your textbook.

1. I'm so busy I don't have time to sleep.

2. Besides soy sauce, there is also sesame oil.

3. The dumpling filling is mainly meat and cabbage.

4. Would you like to go to my place next weekend to eat dumplings?

5. You must be ("certainly are") very thirsty; drink a little beer, how would that be?

Character Practice Sheet

NAME _____ COURSE _____ DATE _____

| 愿 | 一 | 厂 | 厂 | 厂 | 厃 | 厇 | 百 | 原 | 原 | 原 |
| | 原 | 原 | 愿 | 愿 | | | | | | |

当	丨	丷	丷	当	当	当				

| 除 | 了 | 阝 | 阝 | 阝 | 阣 | 除 | 除 | 除 | | |
| | | | | | | | | | | |

| 让 | 丶 | 讠 | 让 | 计 | 让 | | | | | |
| | | | | | | | | | | |

调	丶	讠	讠	讱	调	调	调	调	调	

| 料 | 丶 | 丷 | 丷 | 半 | 半 | 米 | 米 | 米 | 粁 | 料 |
| | | | | | | | | | | |

Reading and Writing Exercises

NAME _____ COURSE _____ DATE _____

A. **Transcribe what you hear in the online audio into Chinese characters.**

(1)

(2)

(3)

B. **If a reference is given after a question, answer based on the referenced part of the Reading Exercises. If no reference is indicated, you may answer any way you wish.**

(1) 除了小林和小方之外，还有别的同学愿意再去动物园吗？A4

(2) 那个女生愿意和那个男生一起吃中饭吗？B1

(3) 你觉得张太太应当怎么办？C2

(4) 如果有人跟你说"让你久等了"，你会怎么跟他说？

Eating with a Colleague in a Restaurant

PART ONE

Listening Comprehension Exercises

NAME _____ COURSE _____ DATE _____

Based on the recorded passages, circle the best response to each of the questions that follow. You may listen to each passage as many times as needed.

EXERCISE ONE: QUESTIONS

1. **Where had the man gone?**

    (A) Bank

    (B) Newspaper kiosk

    (C) Post office

2. **What did the man buy?**

    (A) A dictionary

    (B) A magazine

    (C) A map

3. **What did the woman think of the food in the dining hall?**

    (A) Very tasty

    (B) A little salty

    (C) A little spicy

EXERCISE TWO: QUESTIONS

1. **How is the fish?**

    (A) Very tasty

    (B) Quite tender

    (C) It contains a few too many fish bones.

2. **What course must one of the men teach after lunch?**

    (A) First-year Chinese

    (B) Second-year Chinese

    (C) Third-year Chinese

3. **How much does the meal cost?**

    (A) 26 RMB

    (B) 52 RMB

    (C) 62 RMB

4. **Who is paying for the meal?**

    (A) The same person as last time

    (B) A different person from last time

    (C) They're splitting the bill.

Translation Exercise

NAME _____   COURSE _____   DATE _____

Translate the following sentences into Pinyin romanization with correct tone marks. If you have forgotten a word, consult the English-Chinese Glossary in the back of your textbook.

1. **Have you guys eaten yet?**

2. **I just made up two classes at the cram school.**

3. **The fish is quite tasty, quite tender.** (use **mán...-de**)

4. **A: The check please. B: Let me pay! A: No, today I'm treating.**

5. **The Pockmarked Old Woman's Tofu is very good, it's just a little too spicy hot.**

Character Practice Sheet

NAME _____ COURSE _____ DATE _____

而	一	一	丆	历	而	而			
且	丨	冂	冃	月	且				
鱼	丿	夕	亇	甪	甶	甶	鱼	鱼	
改	乛	乛	己	己	굗	改	改		
务	丿	夕	夂	冬	务				
员	丶	丆	口	吕	吕	员	员		

Reading and Writing Exercises

NAME _____   COURSE _____   DATE _____

A. **Transcribe what you hear in the online audio into Chinese characters.**

(1)

(2)

(3)

B. **If a reference is given after a question, answer based on the referenced part of the Reading Exercises. If no reference is indicated, you may answer any way you wish.**

(1) 说话的那个人要服务员做什么？A5

(2) 那个人的表姐现在还在工厂里工作吗？A6

(3) 和平饭店的服务好吗？B2

(4) 你是喜欢吃牛肉还是喜欢吃鱼？

PART TWO

Listening Comprehension Exercises

NAME _____ COURSE _____ DATE _____

Based on the recorded passages, circle the best response to each of the questions that follow. You may listen to each passage as many times as needed.

EXERCISE ONE: QUESTIONS

1. **How many times has Professor Cohen been to China before this trip?**

    (A) Once

    (B) Twice

    (C) Three times

2. **When was she here last?**

    (A) Last year

    (B) Three years ago

    (C) Five years ago

3. **Who speaks better Chinese?**

    (A) Professor Cohen

    (B) Professor Cohen's husband

    (C) They speak Chinese equally well.

4. **Which of the following is a possible date for Professor Cohen's departure for the U.S.?**

    (A) March 15

    (B) April 15

    (C) May 17

EXERCISE TWO: QUESTIONS

1. **What is going to happen in the evening?**

    (A) A banquet

    (B) A party

    (C) Overtime work

2. **Based on the passage, what is the general manager probably very good at?**

    (A) Chinese cuisine

    (B) Drinking alcohol

    (C) Managing employees

Translation Exercise

NAME _____   COURSE _____   DATE _____

Translate the following sentences into Pinyin romanization with correct tone marks. If you have forgotten a word, consult the English-Chinese Glossary in the back of your textbook.

1.   Showing respect is not so good as following orders.

2.   I've heard that lake is deep, but this river is shallow.

3.   In that case, I'll drink bottoms up first to show respect.

4.   This evening we're having a welcoming dinner for Mr. and Mrs. Smith (use Sī).

5.   My capacity for drinking alcohol is shallow; you drink bottoms up, I'll just have a little.

Character Practice Sheet

NAME _____   COURSE _____   DATE _____

替	一	二	夫	夫	夫一	夫二	扶	扶	扶	替
	替	替								
接	一	十	扌	扩	扩	扩	护	接	接	接
	接									
敢	乛	丆	予	乔	齐	耳	耳	耳	敢	敢
	敢									
量	丨	冂	日	日	旦	昙	昰	昌	昌	量
	量	量								
深	丶	丷	氵	氵	汃	汃	深	深	深	深
	深									
石	一	丆	孑	石	石					

Reading and Writing Exercises

NAME _____ COURSE _____ DATE _____

A. Transcribe what you hear in the online audio into Chinese characters.

(1)

(2)

(3)

B. If a reference is given after a question, answer based on the referenced part of the Reading Exercises. If no reference is indicated, you may answer any way you wish.

(1) 学校前边的河很深，水里应该有很多鱼吧？ A6

(2) 王大海跟他爸爸比起来，谁的酒量比较大？ A10

(3) 为什么那个人要替老简接风？ C2

(4) 你要是去了中国，敢不敢开口跟中国人说中国话？

A Dinner Party at Home
PART ONE

Listening Comprehension Exercises

NAME _____ COURSE _____ DATE _____

Based on the recorded passages, circle the best response to each of the questions that follow. You may listen to each passage as many times as needed.

EXERCISE ONE: QUESTIONS

1. **What kind of a dish did the hostess make especially for the guest?**

   (A) Beef

   (B) Fish

   (C) Pork

2. **What is the most likely relationship between the two speakers?**

   (A) Boss and employee

   (B) Teacher and student

   (C) Host family mother and student

3. **Does the guest allow the hostess to serve her food?**

   (A) Yes, because she can't reach it.

   (B) No, she prefers to help herself.

   (C) She thanks the hostess but says it's not necessary.

EXERCISE TWO: QUESTIONS

1. **Which meal are the two speakers preparing?**

   (A) Breakfast

   (B) Lunch

   (C) Dinner

2. **Which means of transportation is Xiaohang likely to use today?**

   (A) Bus

   (B) Taxi

   (C) Train

3. **How long has Xiaohang been overseas?**

   (A) About one year

   (B) About three years

   (C) About five years

Translation Exercise

NAME _____   COURSE _____   DATE _____

Translate the following sentences into Pinyin romanization with correct tone marks. If you have forgotten a word, consult the English-Chinese Glossary in the back of your textbook.

1.   **I haven't gone there for five or six years.**

2.   **Mr. Wang is wearing a blue shirt.** (use **-zhe**)

3.   **Recently we've been very busy.** (use **-de hěn**)

4.   **She made Sweet and Sour Pork especially for you.**

5.   **The aroma in smelling it is really fragrant.** (use **-zhe**)

Character Practice Sheet

NAME _____ COURSE _____ DATE _____

预	フ	マ	ラ	予	予	予	予	预	预	预
爱	ィ	ィ	ィ	爫	爫	爫	乊	妥	爱	爱
步	丨	卜	止	止	牛	步	步			
数	丶	ハ	ᆢ	半	半	米	米	米	米	米
	数	数	数							
紧	丨	刂	リ	収	坚	坚	紧	紧	紧	
啊	丨	冂	口	叩	叩	啊	啊	啊	啊	

Reading and Writing Exercises

NAME _____ COURSE _____ DATE _____

A. **Transcribe what you hear in the online audio into Chinese characters.**

   (1)

   (2)

   (3)

B. **If a reference is given after a question, answer based on the referenced part of the Reading Exercises. If no reference is indicated, you may answer any way you wish.**

   (1) 今天的天气预报怎么说？ A6

   (2) "饭后百步走，活到九十九"这句话是什么意思？ B2

   (3) 小东的最爱是什么？ C

   (4) 你最近学习紧不紧张？

PART TWO

Listening Comprehension Exercises

NAME _____ COURSE _____ DATE _____

Based on the recorded passages, circle the best response to each of the questions that follow. You may listen to each passage as many times as needed.

EXERCISE ONE: QUESTIONS

1. **What does the woman think of the food in the restaurant where they're now eating?**

    (A) It's outstanding in every possible way.

    (B) It's not as good as in restaurants in China.

    (C) It's not as good as in restaurants in Taiwan.

2. **How often does the woman go to Chinese restaurants in America?**

    (A) Once a week

    (B) Once a month

    (C) Twice a month

3. **Why does she go to Chinese restaurants in America?**

    (A) They're relatively cheap.

    (B) They cook good food.

    (C) She's sometimes homesick.

EXERCISE TWO: QUESTIONS

1. **Where did the meal take place?**

    (A) Company

    (B) Private home

    (C) Restaurant

2. **How many bowls of rice did the speaker eat?**

    (A) One

    (B) Two

    (C) Three

3. **What did the speaker drink during the meal?**

    (A) Beer

    (B) Juice

    (C) Water

Translation Exercise

NAME _____ COURSE _____ DATE _____

Translate the following sentences into Pinyin romanization with correct tone marks. If you have forgotten a word, consult the English-Chinese Glossary in the back of your textbook.

1. I'll substitute tea for wine; here's to you!

2. Although the fruit they sell are cheap, they're not fresh.

3. The food you cooked is too good; not even a restaurant could compare!

4. Everyone please go to the living room and sit down and drink some tea.

5. Though Mrs. Shi is only a substitute teacher, she teaches extremely well.

Character Practice Sheet

NAME _____   COURSE _____   DATE _____

代	ノ	イ	仁	代	代				
课	丶	讠	订	讠门	讠门	讠日	课	课	课
馆	ノ	㇇	乍	𰷣	𰷣	饣门	饣门	饣门	馆
	馆								
虽	丨	冂	口	尸	吕	吕	吊	虽	虽
茶	一	十	艹	艻	艾	芯	芧	茅	茶
乐	ノ	㇄	千	乒	乐				

Reading and Writing Exercises

NAME _____ COURSE _____ DATE _____

A. **Transcribe what you hear in the online audio into Chinese characters.**

(1)

(2)

(3)

B. **If a reference is given after a question, answer based on the referenced part of the Reading Exercises. If no reference is indicated, you may answer any way you wish.**

(1) 小李虽然没钱，可是很快乐，对不对？ A2

(2) 有老师特别喜欢在饭馆儿上课，你觉得有没有关系？

(3) 如果有一个人以茶代酒，那么他最后喝的是茶还是酒？

(4) 可口可乐和百事可乐，你喝得出来哪个是哪个吗？你比较喜欢喝哪个？

LESSON 13
On the Telephone

PART ONE

Listening Comprehension Exercises

NAME _____ COURSE _____ DATE _____

Based on the recorded passages, circle the best response to each of the questions that follow. You may listen to each passage as many times as needed.

EXERCISE ONE: QUESTIONS

1. **What time does the concert start?**
    (A) 7:15 PM
    (B) 7:30 PM
    (C) 8:00 PM

2. **What time does this group of people plan to arrive at the concert hall?**
    (A) 6:45 PM
    (B) 7:15 PM
    (C) 7:30 PM

3. **Is it difficult to acquire extra tickets to the concert?**
    (A) Tickets to the concert are all sold out.
    (B) No, but it would be best to come early.
    (C) Admission to the concert is free.

4. **How many will be in this group of people?**
    (A) Two
    (B) Three
    (C) Four

EXERCISE TWO: QUESTIONS

1. **What has the one man been doing the last few days?**
    (A) Reading
    (B) Taking exams
    (C) Working

2. **Why did one man suggest to the other one that they go to the Great Wall this weekend?**
    (A) So that he can take a rest
    (B) Because the speaker doesn't want to go alone
    (C) Because the other man hasn't been there before

3. **When will they meet on Saturday?**
    (A) 7:00 AM
    (B) 8:00 AM
    (C) 9:00 AM

Translation Exercise

NAME _____   COURSE _____   DATE _____

Translate the following sentences into Pinyin romanization with correct tone marks. If you have forgotten a word, consult the English-Chinese Glossary in the back of your textbook.

1.   **What are you interested in?**

2.   **We're all interested in music.**

3.   **I wonder if you'd be free tomorrow afternoon?**

4.   **I tell you, this Sunday evening there is a concert.**

5.   **These last few weeks really have made me incredibly busy.**   (use **bǎ**)

Character Practice Sheet

NAME _____ COURSE _____ DATE _____

坏	一	十	土	扌	圷	圷	坏	
提	一	十	扌	扫	护	护	捍	捍
	提	提						
际	了	阝	阝	阡	阡	阼	际	
音	丶	一	立	立	立	产	音	音
空	丶	丷	宀	宀	穴	空	空	空
趣	一	十	士	赱	丰	走	走	赵 赵 赵
	趄	趄	趄	趣	趣			

Reading and Writing Exercises

NAME _____ COURSE _____ DATE _____

A. **Transcribe what you hear in the online audio into Chinese characters.**

(1)

(2)

(3)

B. **If a reference is given after a question, answer based on the referenced part of the Reading Exercises. If no reference is indicated, you may answer any way you wish.**

(1) 最近几年，北京的空气怎么样？ A2

(2) 今天晚上的音乐会，我们应该几点钟到比较好？ A6

(3) 你对国际关系感不感兴趣？

(4) 今天晚上有音乐会，不知道你有没有空儿？

PART TWO

Listening Comprehension Exercises

Based on the recorded passages, circle the best response to each of the questions that follow. You may listen to each passage as many times as needed.

EXERCISE ONE: QUESTIONS

1. **What's the name of the travel agency where the caller works?**

   (A) Guó'ān

   (B) Guótài

   (C) Guóxīng

2. **Why wasn't Mr. Li able to come to the phone?**

   (A) Mr. Li was in a meeting.

   (B) Mr. Li was out for lunch.

   (C) Mr. Li was talking to a colleague.

3. **What's the travel agent's extension?**

   (A) 537

   (B) 357

   (C) 375

EXERCISE TWO: QUESTIONS

1. **What will be the local time when the man arrives in Taiwan?**

   (A) 10:00 PM

   (B) 4:00 AM

   (C) 4:00 PM

2. **What is the man's telephone number in Taiwan?**

   (A) 886-86749325

   (B) 886-87649235

   (C) 886-86749253

3. **What is the problem that the man points out?**

   (A) The woman will be sleeping when the man arrives.

   (B) The man doesn't have the woman's telephone number.

   (C) The man won't have access to a cell phone when he arrives.

4. **How do they solve the problem?**

   (A) The woman will call the man.

   (B) The man will call the woman later.

   (C) The woman gives the man her telephone number.

Translation Exercise

Translate the following sentences into Pinyin romanization with correct tone marks. If you have forgotten a word, consult the English-Chinese Glossary in the back of your textbook.

1. Hello? Please transfer me to 2113.

2. They're just in a meeting right now.

3. The minute she gets out of class she returns to her dorm.

4. As soon as they're finished with their meeting, I'll tell them.

5. Extension 2113 is busy; do you want to wait a while or call again later?

Character Practice Sheet

NAME _____ COURSE _____ DATE _____

占	丨	卜	上	占	占					
线	㇄	㇄	纟	纟	纟	线	线	线		
告	丿	𠂉	牛	生	牛	告	告			
诉	丶	讠	讠	讠	诉	诉	诉			
挂	一	十	扌	扩	扩	护	挂	挂	挂	
传	丿	亻	亻	仁	传	传				

Reading and Writing Exercises

NAME _____ COURSE _____ DATE _____

A. **Transcribe what you hear in the online audio into Chinese characters.**

(1)

(2)

(3)

B. **If a reference is given after a question, answer based on the referenced part of the Reading Exercises. If no reference is indicated, you may answer any way you wish.**

(1) 你觉得，文太太为什么挂电话了？ A2

(2) 说话的人要小毛做什么？ A3

(3) 那个人要告诉他妹妹什么？ A6

(4) 要是你给朋友打电话但是电话占线，你怎么办？

Calling About an Ad for an Apartment

PART ONE

NAME _____ COURSE _____ DATE _____

Based on the recorded passages, circle the best response to each of the questions that follow. You may listen to each passage as many times as needed.

EXERCISE ONE: QUESTIONS

1. **How big is the larger of the two bedrooms?**

    (A) 7 ping

    (B) 11 ping

    (C) 29 ping

2. **How many people came to see the apartment yesterday?**

    (A) One person

    (B) Two people

    (C) Five people

3. **When would the landlord be able to show the man the apartment?**

    (A) Friday at 9:00 AM

    (B) Friday at 2:00 PM

    (C) Friday at 4:00 PM

EXERCISE TWO: QUESTIONS

1. **What is the problem at the beginning of the conversation?**

    (A) There is static.

    (B) The volume is too low.

    (C) The man is speaking unclearly.

2. **Why is the young woman interested in the apartment?**

    (A) The rent is reasonable.

    (B) The location is convenient.

    (C) The apartment is quiet.

3. **When is the young woman going to come look at the apartment?**

    (A) Today at 2:00 PM

    (B) Tomorrow at 10:00 AM

    (C) Tomorrow at 3:00 PM

4. **Which of the following is NOT true?**

    (A) The apartment has an area of 25 ping.

    (B) The landlord placed an ad in the newspaper.

    (C) Many people have showed interest in the apartment.

Translation Exercise

NAME _____ COURSE _____ DATE _____

Translate the following sentences into Pinyin romanization with correct tone marks. If you have forgotten a word, consult the English-Chinese Glossary in the back of your textbook.

1. **How big is the kitchen?**

2. **How many bedrooms are there?**

3. **Yesterday I saw their advertisement in the newspaper.**

4. **I wonder if your apartment has been rented out yet or not?**

5. **If you want to come take a look, it would be best to come earlier.**

Character Practice Sheet

NAME _____ COURSE _____ DATE _____

声	一	十	士	吉	吉	吉	声		
立	丶	亠	六	立	立				
红	乚	纟	纟	红	红	红			
黄	一 黄	十	艹	卄	芒	苦	苦	黄	黄
图	丨	冂	冂	冈	图	图	图	图	
领	丿 领	人	亼	今	令	令	令	领	领

Reading and Writing Exercises

NAME _____ COURSE _____ DATE _____

A. **Transcribe what you hear in the online audio into Chinese characters.**

(1)

(2)

(3)

B. **If a reference is given after a question, answer based on the referenced part of the Reading Exercises. If no reference is indicated, you may answer any way you wish.**

(1) 那位美国领事的声调准不准？ A3

(2) 王大海叫我立刻去买什么？ A10

(3) 黄河为什么叫"黄河"？ C1

(4) 你平常是在图书馆学习还是在自己的房间学习？

PART TWO

Listening Comprehension Exercises

NAME _____ COURSE _____ DATE _____

Based on the recorded passages, circle the best response to each of the questions that follow. You may listen to each passage as many times as needed.

EXERCISE ONE: QUESTIONS

1. **Which of the following is available in the apartment?**
   (A) Bed
   (B) Bookcase
   (C) Phone

2. **How much is the deposit?**
   (A) 2500 RMB
   (B) 3500 RMB
   (C) 7000 RMB

3. **When will the prospective tenant come to look at the apartment?**
   (A) In the afternoon of the same day
   (B) In the morning of the next day
   (C) In the afternoon of the next day

4. **How many times has the prospective tenant called the landlord previously?**
   (A) At least once
   (B) At least twice
   (C) More than three times

EXERCISE TWO: QUESTIONS

1. **Based on the passage, what is available in the apartment?**
   (A) Air conditioner
   (B) Telephone
   (C) Furniture

2. **Which of the following is true?**
   (A) The apartment is in a safe neighborhood.
   (B) Someone is currently still living in the apartment.
   (C) The tenant is ready to sign the lease.

3. **When will the apartment become available?**
   (A) June 1
   (B) June 15
   (C) June 30

Translation Exercise

NAME _____ COURSE _____ DATE _____

Translate the following sentences into Pinyin romanization with correct tone marks. If you have forgotten a word, consult the English-Chinese Glossary in the back of your textbook.

1. The deposit is one month's rent.

2. On the wall there is hanging a map of America.

3. The rent is ¥ 3,500 per month, with water and electricity extra.

4. If we arrived this evening at 7:00 or 8:00, would that be convenient?

5. The apartment has some simple furniture like a sofa, desk, closet, and so on. (use **yìxiē**)

Character Practice Sheet

NAME _____ COURSE _____ DATE _____

床	丶	宀	广	庐	庍	床	床		
另	丿	口	口	号	另				
怕	丶	丷	忄	忄	忄	怕	怕	怕	
树	一	十	才	木	朾	权	杈	树	树
花	一	十	艹	艻	花	花	花		
草	一	十	艹	艹	芦	芦	苜	草	草

Reading and Writing Exercises

NAME _____ COURSE _____ DATE _____

A. **Transcribe what you hear in the online audio into Chinese characters.**

(1)

(2)

(3)

B. **If a reference is given after a question, answer based on the referenced part of the Reading Exercises. If no reference is indicated, you may answer any way you wish.**

(1) 为什么有的香港的男人很坏？ A7

(2) 小林为什么早上六点就起床？ B1

(3) 你怕什么？

(4) 你房间里的床是单人床还是双人床？

Visiting a Friend at Home

PART ONE

Listening Comprehension Exercises

NAME _____ COURSE _____ DATE _____

Based on the recorded passages, circle the best response to each of the questions that follow. You may listen to each passage as many times as needed.

EXERCISE ONE: QUESTIONS

1. **Why couldn't the daughter come out to greet the visitor right away?**

   (A) She was in the bathroom.

   (B) She was on the telephone.

   (C) She was busy in the kitchen.

2. **How long was the visitor asked to wait?**

   (A) 5 minutes

   (B) 10 minutes

   (C) 15 minutes

3. **What did the visitor ask to drink?**

   (A) Beer

   (B) Tea

   (C) Water

EXERCISE TWO: QUESTIONS

1. **What do we know about the male speaker's grandfather?**

   (A) He has a beard.

   (B) He's already 80 years old.

   (C) He just celebrated his birthday.

2. **What do we learn from this passage?**

   (A) The male speaker is 17 or over.

   (B) Sophomore year in Chinese high schools is a very busy time.

   (C) The woman hasn't seen the male speaker's sister for seven years.

3. **Which of the following is NOT true about the male speaker's sister?**

   (A) She's very busy with her studies.

   (B) She spends a lot of time on music.

   (C) She has changed a lot in the past several years.

Translation Exercise

NAME _____   COURSE _____   DATE _____

Translate the following sentences into Pinyin romanization with correct tone marks. If you have forgotten a word, consult the English-Chinese Glossary in the back of your textbook.

1. Hello, Uncle! Hello, Auntie!

2. You take your time, don't rush.

3. Please say hello to your parents.

4. Little Li is just shaving; he'll be done in a moment.

5. Children are always unable to stay inside a room, they want to go outside and play.

Character Practice Sheet

NAME _____ COURSE _____ DATE _____

孩	フ	了	孑	孑	孜	孩	孩	孩	孩
马	フ	马	马						
相	一	十	才	木	朼	机	相	相	相
管	ノ	⺮	⺮	⺮	竹	竹	竹	竹	竻	竻
	竻	符	管	管					
严	一	丆	丌	亓	亚	亚	严		
重	一	二	千	台	台	盲	重	重	重

Reading and Writing Exercises

NAME _____ COURSE _____ DATE _____

A. Transcribe what you hear in the online audio into Chinese characters.

(1)

(2)

(3)

B. If a reference is given after a question, answer based on the referenced part of the Reading Exercises. If no reference is indicated, you may answer any way you wish.

(1) 为什么需要马上解决这个问题? A6

(2) 最近几年中美关系怎么样? A8

(3) 作者觉得做爸爸、妈妈的应该管什么? C1

(4) 你以后要不要孩子? 如果你想要的话, 你要几个?

PART TWO

Listening Comprehension Exercises

NAME _____ COURSE _____ DATE _____

Based on the recorded passages, circle the best response to each of the questions that follow. You may listen to each passage as many times as needed.

EXERCISE ONE: QUESTIONS

1. **When the travel agent called the man, what was he doing?**

   (A) Driving

   (B) Taking a cab

   (C) In a meeting

2. **How soon can the man get home?**

   (A) In ten minutes

   (B) In fifteen minutes

   (C) In twenty minutes

3. **What is the travel agent's phone number?**

   (A) 8159-9803

   (B) 8159-9083

   (C) 8759-9083

EXERCISE TWO: QUESTIONS

1. **What will one of the speakers do tomorrow?**

   (A) Spend time with a relative

   (B) Visit a friend

   (C) Go to the Summer Palace

2. **During which season did one of the women most likely go to the Great Wall last time?**

   (A) In the spring

   (B) In the summer

   (C) In the winter

3. **Where will the two women meet on Saturday?**

   (A) At the home of one of the women

   (B) At the relative's home

   (C) At the entrance to the Summer Palace

Translation Exercise

NAME _____   COURSE _____   DATE _____

Translate the following sentences into Pinyin romanization with correct tone marks. If you have forgotten a word, consult the English-Chinese Glossary in the back of your textbook.

1. He studied while eating lunch.

2. Since you still have things to do, I won't keep you.

3. In a little while when we're finished talking, I'll call you.

4. We still want to go out on the street and buy some things.

5. It's getting late ("the time is no longer early"), **I should be going now.**

Character Practice Sheet

NAME _____ COURSE _____ DATE _____

谈	`	讠	讠	讠	讠	谈	谈	谈	谈	谈
既	7	⼸	⺕	⻏	艮	既	既	既		
送	`	⺊	⺍	兰	关	关	送	送		
使	ノ	亻	仁	仃	仨	佢	使	使		
希	ノ	乄	产	羊	羊	希	希			
望	`	⺀	亡	亣	切	胡	胡	望	望	望
	望									

Reading and Writing Exercises

NAME _____ COURSE _____ DATE _____

A. Transcribe what you hear in the online audio into Chinese characters.

(1)

(2)

(3)

B. If a reference is given after a question, answer based on the referenced part of the Reading Exercises. If no reference is indicated, you may answer any way you wish.

(1) 张先生打算改天做什么？ A7

(2) 既然饭馆的菜不怎么样，他们就决定做什么了？ A8

(3) 一位大使在哪儿工作？ 一位领事呢？

(4) 你的生日那天，你希望朋友们送给你什么东西？

Calling on Someone to Request a Favor

PART ONE

Listening Comprehension Exercises

NAME _____ COURSE _____ DATE _____

Based on the recorded passages, circle the best response to each of the questions that follow. You may listen to each passage as many times as needed.

EXERCISE ONE: QUESTIONS

1. **When does this conversation take place?**
    (A) 11:30 AM
    (B) 2:30 PM
    (C) 5:50 PM

2. **Why did the woman come to see the man and his wife?**
    (A) To ask for a favor
    (B) To show her appreciation for their help
    (C) To thank the man for his excellent teaching

3. **What does the woman do before leaving?**
    (A) Take out a gift
    (B) Invite the couple to lunch
    (C) Invite the couple to visit her in the U.S.

EXERCISE TWO: QUESTIONS

1. **What time is the man going to depart for Hong Kong?**
    (A) 9:30 PM
    (B) 10:45 PM
    (C) 2:40 PM

2. **How long does it take to fly to Hong Kong?**
    (A) About two hours
    (B) About three hours
    (C) About four hours

3. **Why does the woman want the man to buy a computer in Hong Kong?**
    (A) Hong Kong has the model she wants.
    (B) Merchandise in Hong Kong is often cheaper than in China.
    (C) The quality of merchandise in Hong Kong is higher than in China.

4. **For whom is the computer?**
    (A) For the woman's boyfriend
    (B) For the woman's father
    (C) For the woman's younger sister

Translation Exercise

NAME _____ COURSE _____ DATE _____

Translate the following sentences into Pinyin romanization with correct tone marks. If you have forgotten a word, consult the English-Chinese Glossary in the back of your textbook.

1. Mrs. Wang, this is a little something for you.

2. A: Please have a cigarette! B: I don't smoke, thanks.

3. I feel the custom of taking off one's shoes is very good.

4. There is a little matter I'd like to request that you help with.

5. Sorry, because at the last minute there was a little something, I came late.

Character Practice Sheet

NAME _____ COURSE _____ DATE _____

抽	一	寸	扌	扣	扣	扣	抽	抽	
烟	丶	丷	少	火	灯	灯	炳	烟	烟
吸	丨	冂	口	叻	吸	吸			
区	一	丆	叉	区					
情	丶	丷	忄	忄	忄	忄	忄	情	情
	情								
帮	一	二	三	丰	邦	邦	邦	帮	帮

Reading and Writing Exercises

NAME _____ COURSE _____ DATE _____

A. **Transcribe what you hear in the online audio into Chinese characters.**

(1)

(2)

(3)

B. **If a reference is given after a question, answer based on the referenced part of the Reading Exercises. If no reference is indicated, you may answer any way you wish.**

(1) 有的时候中国人对不可能的事情会怎么样？ C1

(2) 作者特别不喜欢的事情是什么？ C2

(3) 你抽不抽烟？

(4) 如果有一个好朋友来找你，对你说："有点小事情，想请你帮个忙"，你会怎么说？

PART TWO

Listening Comprehension Exercises

NAME _____ COURSE _____ DATE _____

Based on the recorded passages, circle the best response to each of the questions that follow. You may listen to each passage as many times as needed.

EXERCISE ONE: QUESTIONS

1. **By when will the man be able to get back to the woman?**
   (A) By next Wednesday
   (B) By next Saturday
   (C) By next Sunday

2. **What's the woman's phone number?**
   (A) 2463-8952
   (B) 2643-9825
   (C) 2643-8925

3. **Around what time of day does this conversation take place?**
   (A) 11:30 AM
   (B) 2:30 PM
   (C) 5:30 PM

EXERCISE TWO: QUESTIONS

1. **What do we know about this apartment?**
   (A) The apartment is furnished.
   (B) Water and electricity are included in the rent.
   (C) It's O.K. if the female speaker wants to have a roommate.

2. **How much is the deposit for one person?**
   (A) 1500 RMB
   (B) 1700 RMB
   (C) 3000 RMB

3. **How does this conversation conclude?**
   (A) The prospective tenant decides to rent the apartment.
   (B) The prospective tenant decides not to rent the apartment.
   (C) The prospective tenant needs more time to consider the matter.

Translation Exercise

NAME _____   COURSE _____   DATE _____

Translate the following sentences into Pinyin romanization with correct tone marks. If you have forgotten a word, consult the English-Chinese Glossary in the back of your textbook.

1.   Oh, that's right, I just thought of something.

2.   Some other day I'll come again to pay a call on you.

3.   This matter, I'll do my best to help you find out about it.

4.   If by chance it's not easy to inquire about, don't try too hard.

5.   At the latest we'll give you an answer by next Monday, all right?

Character Practice Sheet

NAME _____ COURSE _____ DATE _____

容	⟍	⟋⟍	宀	宀	穴	宓	突	容	容
易	⎺	冂	冃	日	尸	昜	易	易	
尽	⎺	尸	尸	尺	尺	尽			
力	フ	力							
化	ノ	亻	亻	化					
流	⟍	⟍⟍	氵	氵	汸	汸	流	流	流

Reading and Writing Exercises

NAME _____ COURSE _____ DATE _____

A. **Transcribe what you hear in the online audio into Chinese characters.**

(1)

(2)

(3)

B. **If a reference is given after a question, answer based on the referenced part of the Reading Exercises. If no reference is indicated, you may answer any way you wish.**

(1) 说话的那个人保证什么？ A2

(2) 那位中国女同学对什么特别感兴趣？ C2

(3) 她想找一位日本女同学做什么？ C2

(4) 中文学起来很容易吧?

LESSON 17
Visiting a Sick Classmate
PART ONE

Listening Comprehension Exercises

NAME _____ COURSE _____ DATE _____

Based on the recorded passages, circle the best response to each of the questions that follow. You may listen to each passage as many times as needed.

EXERCISE ONE: QUESTIONS

1. **Why does the young man visit his teacher?**

    (A) To thank her

    (B) To ask a favor

    (C) To show his concern

2. **What does the young man bring his teacher?**

    (A) Grapes

    (B) Oranges

    (C) Peaches

3. **When did the young man take his Chinese mid-term exam?**

    (A) This afternoon

    (B) Yesterday morning

    (C) Yesterday afternoon

4. **When will the young man probably see his teacher next?**

    (A) Monday

    (B) Thursday

    (C) Friday

EXERCISE TWO: QUESTIONS

1. **What can be inferred about the man referred to?**

    (A) He's a businessman.

    (B) He's a big spender.

    (C) He's a restaurant manager.

2. **Why will the one woman probably be able to receive a discount at the restaurant?**

    (A) She has a discount coupon.

    (B) She's related to the restaurant manager.

    (C) The other woman has connections at the restaurant.

3. **How much of a discount will she probably receive?**

    (A) 10% off

    (B) 15% off

    (C) 25% off

Translation Exercise

NAME _____ COURSE _____ DATE _____

Translate the following sentences into Pinyin romanization with correct tone marks. If you have forgotten a word, consult the English-Chinese Glossary in the back of your textbook.

1. I'm sick; I'm a little dizzy.

2. He goes running every day.

3. I should have come see you a long time ago.

4. These last few weeks I've been very busy and never had time.

5. The parents are busy earning money; the children are busy spending money.

Character Practice Sheet

NAME _____ COURSE _____ DATE _____

考	一	十	土	耂	老	考			
试	丶	讠	讠	讠	讠	讠	试	试	
病	丶	亠	广	疒	疒	疒	疒	病	病
跑	丨	口	口	甲	甲	甲	足	趵	跑	跑
	跑	跑							
飞	乁	飞	飞						
船	丶	丿	几	凢	舟	舟	舟	船	船	船
	船								

Reading and Writing Exercises

NAME _____ COURSE _____ DATE _____

A. **Transcribe what you hear in the online audio into Chinese characters.**

(1)

(2)

(3)

B. **If a reference is given after a question, answer based on the referenced part of the Reading Exercises. If no reference is indicated, you may answer any way you wish.**

(1) 王明力为什么决定这次要坐船？ B2

(2) 你常生病吗？

(3) 你怕不怕考试？

(4) 你每天都跑步吗？

PART TWO

Listening Comprehension Exercises

NAME _____ COURSE _____ DATE _____

Based on the recorded passages, circle the best response to each of the questions that follow. You may listen to each passage as many times as needed.

EXERCISE ONE: QUESTIONS

1. **What is the main reason the woman calls her son?**

    (A) She's concerned about his health.

    (B) She wants to check up on his studies.

    (C) She wants to update him about matters at home.

2. **Which of the following is NOT true?**

    (A) The young man likes to run.

    (B) Not much has changed with the young man's parents.

    (C) The young man is going to take five courses this term.

3. **What's up with the young man's sister?**

    (A) She's resting.

    (B) She's going to call soon.

    (C) She's applying to college.

EXERCISE TWO: QUESTIONS

1. **What do we know about the speaker?**

    (A) He's busy writing a thesis.

    (B) He's sick and hasn't been to school for a week.

    (C) He thinks his studies are the most important thing in his life.

2. **When did the speaker get sick?**

    (A) Last semester

    (B) Last month

    (C) Last week

3. **What is NOT true?**

    (A) The man is taking 16 credits.

    (B) The man is taking five courses.

    (C) The man has a job at the college library.

4. **Why does the speaker wish he could graduate immediately?**

    (A) He wouldn't have to study anymore.

    (B) He wouldn't have to take tests anymore.

    (C) He wouldn't have to write papers anymore.

Translation Exercise

NAME _____ COURSE _____ DATE _____

Translate the following sentences into Pinyin romanization with correct tone marks. If you have forgotten a word, consult the English-Chinese Glossary in the back of your textbook.

1. **Speak slowly, don't get anxious.**

2. **Why don't you eat with us first before leaving?**

3. **You rest well; pay more attention to your health!**

4. **Come visit us** ("have fun") **again some other day!**

5. **This semester I chose four classes, a total of 16 credits.**

Character Practice Sheet

NAME _____ COURSE _____ DATE _____

身	′	′	′⺈	臽	身	身			
体	′	亻	亻	什	仕	休	体		
绩	′	乡	乡	纟	纟	纩	结	结	绩
绩									
注	`	⺀	氵	氵	泸	泸	汁	注	
于	⼀	二	于						
论	`	讠	讠	论	论	论			

Reading and Writing Exercises

NAME _____ COURSE _____ DATE _____

A. **Transcribe what you hear in the online audio into Chinese characters.**

(1)

(2)

(3)

B. **If a reference is given after a question, answer based on the referenced part of the Reading Exercises. If no reference is indicated, you may answer any way you wish.**

(1) 学中文的学生一定得注意什么？ A3

(2) 小严的论文是关于什么的？ B3

(3) 你身体好吗？

(4) 你上高中的时候，成绩不错吧？

A Farewell Call on a Favorite Teacher

PART ONE

Listening Comprehension Exercises

NAME _____ COURSE _____ DATE _____

Based on the recorded passages, circle the best response to each of the questions that follow. You may listen to each passage as many times as needed.

EXERCISE ONE: QUESTIONS

1. **How long has the male speaker been at the educational institution in question?**

    (A) A month

    (B) A semester

    (C) A year

2. **Which aspect of his Chinese is the male speaker still not satisfied with?**

    (A) Grammar

    (B) Pronunciation

    (C) Vocabulary

3. **Which of the following is NOT a reason that the male speaker came to see the female speaker?**

    (A) He wants to thank her.

    (B) He wants to say goodbye.

    (C) He wants to report his progress in learning Chinese.

EXERCISE TWO: QUESTIONS

1. **What do we know about the female speaker?**

    (A) She's not very used to living in China.

    (B) She's satisfied with her progress in Chinese.

    (C) She has been living in China for less than two years.

2. **What does the woman like most in Beijing?**

    (A) Going out with friends

    (B) Eating at small restaurants

    (C) Chatting with local people

3. **What does the man NOT say about the woman's Chinese?**

    (A) Her Chinese is quite fluent.

    (B) Her pronunciation is not very standard.

    (C) She doesn't yet have enough vocabulary.

Translation Exercise

NAME _____ COURSE _____ DATE _____

Translate the following sentences into Pinyin romanization with correct tone marks. If you have forgotten a word, consult the English-Chinese Glossary in the back of your textbook.

1. **This matter, even they know.**

2. **There have come some guests.**

3. **Gosh, time passes really quickly!**

4. **I've come to bid farewell to you all.**

5. **He can't write even one Chinese character**

Character Practice Sheet

NAME _____ COURSE _____ DATE _____

向	′	亻	门	向	向	向		
眼	丨	冂	冃	月	目	目	盯	目 眼
眼								
连	一	左	左	车	车	许	连	
利	′	二	千	千	禾	利	利	
产	丶	亠	亠	立	立	产		
义	丶	丷	义					

Reading and Writing Exercises

NAME _____ COURSE _____ DATE _____

A. Transcribe what you hear in the online audio into Chinese characters.

(1)

(2)

(3)

B. If a reference is given after a question, answer based on the referenced part of the Reading Exercises. If no reference is indicated, you may answer any way you wish.

(1) 请你提三种主义。A7

(2) 这位女生的男朋友告诉她他交了别的女朋友，讲完话以后，有没有看她一眼？C1

(3) 你的中文讲得很流利吧？

(4) 你是比较内向的人还是比较外向的人？

PART TWO

Listening Comprehension Exercises

NAME _____ COURSE _____ DATE _____

Based on the recorded passages, circle the best response to each of the questions that follow. You may listen to each passage as many times as needed.

EXERCISE ONE: QUESTIONS

1. **How many years did the student study Chinese before going to China?**

   (A) Two and one-half years

   (B) Three and one-half years

   (C) Four and one-half years

2. **What is the student supposed to do after his return to his native country?**

   (A) Convey greetings

   (B) Study Chinese

   (C) Write letters

3. **Which of the following is NOT true?**

   (A) The student is busy with his final exams right now.

   (B) The student has made rapid progress in his study of Chinese.

   (C) The student will continue to study Chinese after he goes back to his country.

EXERCISE TWO: QUESTIONS

1. **Why did the male speaker initiate the conversation?**

   (A) He wants to send a postcard.

   (B) He wants to send a parcel.

   (C) He wants to know the business hours of the post office.

2. **When does the post office open tomorrow?**

   (A) 8:00 AM

   (B) 8:30 AM

   (C) 9:00 AM

3. **How long does it take for what he asks about to get to the U.S.?**

   (A) About one week

   (B) About two weeks

   (C) About eight weeks

Translation Exercise

NAME _____ COURSE _____ DATE _____

Translate the following sentences into Pinyin romanization with correct tone marks. If you have forgotten a word, consult the English-Chinese Glossary in the back of your textbook.

1. **Send my regards to your Chinese teacher!**

2. **Don't forget to send me a letter when you have time.**

3. **Actually, this is all the result of you yourself being hard-working.**

4. **Excuse me, if I send this letter by airmail, how much in stamps should I stick on it?**

5. **If I hadn't lived in China for a year, I wouldn't have been able to progress so quickly.**

Character Practice Sheet

NAME _____ COURSE _____ DATE _____

责	一	二	丰	主	韦	青	责	责	
任	丿	亻	仁	仁	仟	任			
父	丿	八	夕	父					
母	L	口	口	母	母				
教	一	十	土	耂	芳	孝	孝	孝	教
	教								
信	丿	亻	亻	亻	信	信	信	信	信

Reading and Writing Exercises

NAME_____   COURSE_____   DATE_____

A. **Transcribe what you hear in the online audio into Chinese characters.**

(1)

(2)

(3)

B. **If a reference is given after a question, answer based on the referenced part of the Reading Exercises. If no reference is indicated, you may answer any way you wish.**

(1) 任万里的父母在哪儿教书？ C1

(2) 作者的父母尽了父母应尽的责任吗？ C2

(3) 你常给父母写信吗？

(4) 父母当然对孩子有责任，你相信孩子对父母也有责任吗？

Hobbies

PART ONE

Listening Comprehension Exercises

NAME _____ COURSE _____ DATE _____

Based on the recorded passages, circle the best response to each of the questions that follow. You may listen to each passage as many times as needed.

EXERCISE ONE: QUESTIONS

1. **Why does the man go to the library almost every day?**

    (A) He loves to read.

    (B) His dorm is too noisy.

    (C) He does homework there.

2. **What does the man like to do in his spare time?**

    (A) Paint

    (B) Play Go

    (C) Visit museums

3. **What does the woman like to do in her spare time?**

    (A) Paint

    (B) Read

    (C) Sing

4. **How long has the woman studied piano?**

    (A) 1 year

    (B) 10 years

    (C) 11 years

EXERCISE TWO: QUESTIONS

1. **What is the man's hobby?**

    (A) Painting

    (B) Singing

    (C) Playing the piano

2. **What is the woman's hobby?**

    (A) Painting

    (B) Singing

    (C) Playing the piano

3. **What would the woman like to do?**

    (A) Visit the male speaker's dorm

    (B) Hang paintings on her dorm wall

    (C) Buy a painting from the male speaker

Translation Exercise

NAME _____ COURSE _____ DATE _____

Translate the following sentences into Pinyin romanization with correct tone marks. If you have forgotten a word, consult the English-Chinese Glossary in the back of your textbook.

1. He eats very little; no wonder he's so thin.

2. I've been learning to paint since I was little.

3. When we have time, we like to visit museums.

4. Every evening she reads for two or three hours.

5. Besides singing, do you have any other hobbies?

Character Practice Sheet

NAME _____ COURSE _____ DATE _____

唱	丨	冂	口	口'	口冂	口月	口月	唱	唱	唱
	唱									

歌	一	丆	可	可	可	可	哥	哥	哥	
	哥	歌	歌	歌						

怪	'	丷	忄	忄	忄	怪	怪	怪		

观	刁	又	如	观	观	观				

画	一	丆	丙	石	雨	画	画	画		

照	丨	冂	日	日	日刁	日刀	日刀	昭	昭	昭
	照	照	照							

Reading and Writing Exercises

NAME _____ COURSE _____ DATE _____

A. **Transcribe what you hear in the online audio into Chinese characters.**

(1)

(2)

(3)

B. **If a reference is given after a question, answer based on the referenced part of the Reading Exercises. If no reference is indicated, you may answer any way you wish.**

(1) 那个人的爱好是什么？ A1

(2) 他们要参观什么样的工厂？ A5

(3) 你喜欢不喜欢画画儿？

(4) 你唱歌儿唱得怎么样？

PART TWO

Listening Comprehension Exercises

NAME _____ COURSE _____ DATE _____

Based on the recorded passages, circle the best response to each of the questions that follow. You may listen to each passage as many times as needed.

EXERCISE ONE: QUESTIONS

1. **How many people are going to see Peking Opera?**

    (A) Two people

    (B) Three people

    (C) Four people

2. **Why did the female speaker ask if she could bring her roommate to the show?**

    (A) The male speaker has an extra ticket.

    (B) Her roommate is interested in Peking Opera.

    (C) She and her roommate want to treat the male speaker to dinner.

3. **When will they meet on Saturday?**

    (A) Before 5:00 PM

    (B) At 5:00 PM

    (C) After 5:00 PM

4. **Where will they meet on Saturday?**

    (A) At the man's dormitory

    (B) At the woman's dormitory

    (C) At the entrance to the theater

EXERCISE TWO: QUESTIONS

1. **What kind of event is being discussed?**

    (A) Concert

    (B) Dinner

    (C) Meeting

2. **How many students went to this event?**

    (A) About one-fourth of them

    (B) About one-third of them

    (C) About two-thirds of them

3. **Why did the rest of the students not go?**

    (A) They had class.

    (B) They were busy with exams.

    (C) They're not interested in that kind of event.

4. **When did the male speaker finish his exams?**

    (A) Last Monday

    (B) Last Tuesday

    (C) Last Wednesday

Translation Exercise

NAME _____ COURSE _____ DATE _____

Translate the following sentences into Pinyin romanization with correct tone marks. If you have forgotten a word, consult the English-Chinese Glossary in the back of your textbook.

1. She has great expertise in painting.

2. Only about 20% of the students came.

3. It just happens I have two extra tickets.

4. Three-fourths of my classmates didn't go.

5. People's Theater is 3.8 kilometers from Tian'anmen. (**gōnglǐ** "kilometer")

Character Practice Sheet

NAME _____ COURSE _____ DATE _____

研	一	一	丆	石	石	矴	研	研	研
究	丶	丷	宀	宀	穴	究	究		
懂	丶	丷	忄	忄	忄	忄	忄	忄	惜
惜	惜	懂	懂	懂					
民	一	一	尸	尸	民				
华	丿	亻	亻	化	华	华			
亲	丶	亠	亠	亠	立	辛	辛	亲	亲

Reading and Writing Exercises

NAME _____ COURSE _____ DATE _____

A. Transcribe what you hear in the online audio into Chinese characters.

(1)

(2)

(3)

B. If a reference is given after a question, answer based on the referenced part of the Reading Exercises. If no reference is indicated, you may answer any way you wish.

(1) 中华人民共和国的第一大报叫什么？A1

(2) 华国树的母亲对什么很有研究？A2

(3) 你的父母亲住在哪里？

(4) 中文报纸你看得懂吗？

Going to the Movies

PART ONE

Listening Comprehension Exercises

NAME _____ COURSE _____ DATE _____

Based on the recorded passages, circle the best response to each of the questions that follow. You may listen to each passage as many times as needed.

EXERCISE ONE: QUESTIONS

1. **What is the woman doing when the passage begins?**
   (A) Reading
   (B) Studying
   (C) Her homework

2. **How are the two speakers going to get to the movie theater?**
   (A) Take the bus
   (B) Take a taxi
   (C) Walk

3. **How long will it take them to get to the movie theater?**
   (A) 10 minutes
   (B) 20 minutes
   (C) 30 minutes

4. **Which of the following statements about the movie is true?**
   (A) It's a Chinese film.
   (B) It was recently released.
   (C) It's considered to be a very good film.

EXERCISE TWO: QUESTIONS

1. **What is the movie about?**
   (A) A famous banker
   (B) A famous musician
   (C) A famous novelist

2. **What did the female speaker originally want to be?**
   (A) A banker
   (B) A doctor
   (C) A musician

Translation Exercise

NAME _____   COURSE _____   DATE _____

Translate the following sentences into Pinyin romanization with correct tone marks. If you have forgotten a word, consult the English-Chinese Glossary in the back of your textbook.

1. **Are there any good films recently?**

2. **Would you like to go see a movie with us?**

3. **A: What are you doing? B: Painting.** (for "do" use **gàn**)

4. **What that film is telling is the story of a famous novelist in 1940s China.**

5. **He said there was less crime in the America of the 1950s** ("public security relatively good").

Character Practice Sheet

NAME _____ COURSE _____ DATE _____

影									
	丨	冂	日	日	早	早	异	昌	昙
	景	景	影	影	影				

新									
	丶	亠	立	卒	立	辛	亲	亲	亲
	新	新	新						

故									
	一	十	古	古	古	古	古	故	

将									
	丶	丷	爿	丬	护	护	将	将	将

计									
	丶	讠	订	计					

划									
	一	七	戈	戈	划	划			

Reading and Writing Exercises

NAME _____ COURSE _____ DATE _____

A. **Transcribe what you hear in the online audio into Chinese characters.**

(1)

(2)

(3)

B. **If a reference is given after a question, answer based on the referenced part of the Reading Exercises. If no reference is indicated, you may answer any way you wish.**

(1) 今晚的电影是关于什么？ A4

(2) 王大海最怕什么？ 为什么？ A10

(3) 你将来有什么计划？

(4) 你比较喜欢自己说故事，还是比较喜欢听别人说故事？

PART TWO

Listening Comprehension Exercises

NAME _____ COURSE _____ DATE _____

Based on the recorded passages, circle the best response to each of the questions that follow. You may listen to each passage as many times as needed.

EXERCISE ONE: QUESTIONS

1. **What time does the movie start?**

    (A) 8:00 PM

    (B) 8:15 PM

    (C) 8:30 PM

2. **Where are the two speakers' seats?**

    (A) Downstairs, row 12

    (B) Downstairs, row 22

    (C) Upstairs, row 21

3. **Why isn't the male speaker interested in the film?**

    (A) Because the movie is about a painter

    (B) Because the movie's plot is too "touching"

    (C) Because he doesn't like comedies

EXERCISE TWO: QUESTIONS

1. **What kind of films does the male speaker like to watch?**

    (A) Old black and white films

    (B) Chinese films from the 1980s and 1990s

    (C) Films with the actor Zhou Runfa

2. **What proportion of the language in a Chinese film can the male speaker understand?**

    (A) One-third

    (B) One-half

    (C) Two-thirds

3. **How many Chinese films has the male speaker seen?**

    (A) About 30

    (B) About 40

    (C) About 50

Translation Exercise

NAME _____ COURSE _____ DATE _____

Translate the following sentences into Pinyin romanization with correct tone marks. If you have forgotten a word, consult the English-Chinese Glossary in the back of your textbook.

1. She had never seen that kind of film before.

2. Where is the movie theater? What time is the film shown?

3. The seats are pretty good: upstairs, row 1, numbers 8 and 10.

4. The main content of the film, were you able to understand all of it?

5. In some places they spoke unclearly and I couldn't understand very well.

Character Practice Sheet

NAME _____ COURSE _____ DATE _____

类	丶	丷	丷	半	米	米	丵	丵	类
排	一	十	扌	扌	扫	扫	挑	排	排
排									
楼	一	十	才	木	术	杉	柈	栏	栏
楼 楼 楼									
部	丶	一	亠	立	立	音	音	咅	部
理	一	二	干	王	珏	玑	珇	理	理
理									
它	丶	丷	宀	宁	它				

Reading and Writing Exercises

NAME _____ COURSE _____ DATE _____

A. **Transcribe what you hear in the online audio into Chinese characters.**

(1)

(2)

(3)

B. **If a reference is given after a question, answer based on the referenced part of the Reading Exercises. If no reference is indicated, you may answer any way you wish.**

(1) 那个人忘了什么？ A1

(2) 美国老一代的华人，大部分是从中国什么地方来的？ A4

(3) 那三个人决定学什么专业？

(4) 你住的房间在几楼？

Talking About Sports

PART ONE

Listening Comprehension Exercises

NAME _____ COURSE _____ DATE _____

Based on the recorded passages, circle the best response to each of the questions that follow. You may listen to each passage as many times as needed.

EXERCISE ONE: QUESTIONS

1. **What does the male speaker like to do for exercise?**
   (A) Play badminton
   (B) Play tennis
   (C) Swim

2. **When does the male speaker practice kung fu?**
   (A) Almost every morning
   (B) Every Wednesday
   (C) Every weekend

3. **What does the female speaker do for exercise?**
   (A) Play tennis
   (B) Run
   (C) Swim

4. **When does she usually do this?**
   (A) Almost every morning
   (B) Every Wednesday
   (C) In the evening

EXERCISE TWO: QUESTIONS

1. **Where will the two speakers go jogging?**
   (A) In a park
   (B) At school
   (C) On the street

2. **Why don't they go jogging at night?**
   (A) The female speaker thinks it's not safe.
   (B) The male speaker has homework he must do.
   (C) The male speaker has an evening class at that time.

3. **In the end, what time do they decide to go jogging?**
   (A) Tomorrow morning
   (B) The day after tomorrow in the morning
   (C) On the weekend

Translation Exercise

NAME _____ COURSE _____ DATE _____

Translate the following sentences into Pinyin romanization with correct tone marks. If you have forgotten a word, consult the English-Chinese Glossary in the back of your textbook.

1. I like basketball and tennis; which sports do you like?

2. Before, when I was in Beijing, I often played badminton.

3. Did you learn some different sports, for example, practicing taiji?

4. In the past when I was in college, I was on the school baseball team.

5. You want us to speak only Chinese, but you yourself on the contrary speak English!

Character Practice Sheet

NAME _____ COURSE _____ DATE _____

球	一	二	于	王	王	对	对	球	球
	球								
队	了	阝	队	队					
运	一	二	云	云	云	运	运		
功	一	丁	工	功	功				
室	丶	八	宀	宀	宁	室	宰	室	
倒	丿	亻	亻	任	任	任	任	倒	倒

Reading and Writing Exercises

NAME _____ COURSE _____ DATE _____

A. **Transcribe what you hear in the online audio into Chinese characters.**

(1)

(2)

(3)

B. **If a reference is given after a question, answer based on the referenced part of the Reading Exercises. If no reference is indicated, you may answer any way you wish.**

(1) 王大海用不用功？他妹妹呢？ A10

(2) 儿子原来打算到哪里去做什么？ B2

(3) 你喜欢做哪些运动？

(4) 你这个学期有没有室友？

PART TWO

Listening Comprehension Exercises

NAME _____ COURSE _____ DATE _____

Based on the recorded passages, circle the best response to each of the questions that follow. You may listen to each passage as many times as needed.

EXERCISE ONE: QUESTIONS

1. **Why did the man go to Taiwan during the summer break?**

    (A) To learn taiji

    (B) To study Chinese

    (C) To visit a family member

2. **At what time in the morning did the man practice taiji when he was in Taiwan?**

    (A) 5:00 AM

    (B) 6:00 AM

    (C) 7:00 AM

3. **Why don't more young people in Taiwan practice taiji?**

    (A) They're too busy.

    (B) They think it's too slow.

    (C) They can't get up so early.

4. **What is the man's regret?**

    (A) He's forgetting his taiji.

    (B) He misses his friends in Taiwan.

    (C) Too few young people like taiji.

EXERCISE TWO: QUESTIONS

1. **What does the male speaker want?**

    (A) He wants a vacation.

    (B) He wants to be excused from class.

    (C) He needs time to prepare for his mid-term exam.

2. **Why?**

    (A) He is sick.

    (B) He needs to go to New York City to visit a family member.

    (C) He is tired.

3. **When will the male speaker take his mid-term exam?**

    (A) Next Monday

    (B) Next Tuesday

    (C) Next Wednesday

Translation Exercise

NAME _____ COURSE _____ DATE _____

Translate the following sentences into Pinyin romanization with correct tone marks. If you have forgotten a word, consult the English-Chinese Glossary in the back of your textbook.

1.   **Where shall we meet tomorrow morning?**

2.   **To get up at 5:00 AM is too early for them.**

3.   **Would you be interested in going jogging with me?**

4.   **Don't tell me that Chinese young people all dislike watching Beijing opera?**

5.   **Most middle-aged and older people prefer going walking in the countryside.**

Character Practice Sheet

NAME _____ COURSE _____ DATE _____

假	丿	亻	仆	仆	仴	作	佲	佲	假
	假								
春	一	二	三	声	夫	夫	春	春	
整	一	厂	同	同	申	束	束	敕	敕	敕
	敕	整	整	整	整	整			
育	丶	亠	云	云	云	育	育	育	
社	丶	㇇	㇏	礻	衤	社	社		
团	丨	冂	月	用	团	团			

Reading and Writing Exercises

NAME _____ COURSE _____ DATE _____

A. Transcribe what you hear in the online audio into Chinese characters.

(1)

(2)

(3)

B. If a reference is given after a question, answer based on the referenced part of the Reading Exercises. If no reference is indicated, you may answer any way you wish.

(1) 那个人的室友加入了几个社团？你加入了几个？ A9

(2) 王大海的专业是教育吗？ A10

(3) 女儿为什么最近每天都早上十点才起床？ B2

(4) 假如你有一百万元的话，你会怎么花？

Soccer and an Excursion to the Great Wall

PART ONE

Listening Comprehension Exercises

NAME _____ COURSE _____ DATE _____

Based on the recorded passages, circle the best response to each of the questions that follow. You may listen to each passage as many times as needed.

EXERCISE ONE: QUESTIONS

1. **On what channel is the basketball game?**

   (A) Channel 17

   (B) Channel 20

   (C) Channel 27

2. **What was the score when they turned on the TV?**

   (A) 7 to 14

   (B) 9 to 13

   (C) 9 to 15

3. **How much of the game had they missed when they started watching?**

   (A) 10 minutes

   (B) 20 minutes

   (C) 30 minutes

4. **Which team does the last speaker predict will win the game?**

   (A) Houston Rockets

   (B) Utah Jazz

   (C) He isn't sure.

EXERCISE TWO: QUESTIONS

1. **What kind of television programs does the woman like to watch?**

   (A) Comedies

   (B) Soap operas

   (C) Variety shows

2. **What kind of programs does the woman NOT like to watch?**

   (A) News

   (B) Soap operas

   (C) Sports competitions

3. **What do you think is her favorite American television show?**

   (A) *Friends*

   (B) *Grey's Anatomy*

   (C) *Lost*

Translation Exercise

NAME _____ COURSE _____ DATE _____

Translate the following sentences into Pinyin romanization with correct tone marks. If you have forgotten a word, consult the English-Chinese Glossary in the back of your textbook.

1. **What TV programs do you like to watch?**

2. **Just now it was 5 to 4; now it's 5 to 5 tied.**

3. **Picasso (Bìjiāsuǒ) is a world-famous painter.**

4. **A: Who do you think can win? B: Whoever is lucky will win.**

5. **A: Which team is playing against which team? B: Germany against Spain.**

Character Practice Sheet

NAME _____ COURSE _____ DATE _____

世	一	十	卅	廿	世				
界	丿	冂	田	田	田	甲	界	界	界
目	丨	冂	月	月	目				
视	丶	ラ	礻	礻	礻	初	视	视	
强	ㄱ	ㄱ	弓	弓	弨	弨	弨	强	强
	强	强							
足	丶	口	口	무	무	足	足		

Reading and Writing Exercises

NAME _____ COURSE _____ DATE _____

A. **Transcribe what you hear in the online audio into Chinese characters.**

(1)

(2)

(3)

B. **If a reference is given after a question, answer based on the referenced part of the Reading Exercises. If no reference is indicated, you may answer any way you wish.**

(1) 哪个足球队比较强？ A3

(2) 黄河是世界上最长的河吗？ A7

(3) 你喜欢看足球吗？

(4) 你最喜欢看的电视节目是哪个？

PART TWO

Listening Comprehension Exercises

NAME _____ COURSE _____ DATE _____

Based on the recorded passages, circle the best response to each of the questions that follow. You may listen to each passage as many times as needed.

EXERCISE ONE: QUESTIONS

1. **What will the weather be like tomorrow?**

   (A) Rainy

   (B) Snowy

   (C) Windy

2. **When did the construction of the Forbidden City begin?**

   (A) 1406

   (B) 1420

   (C) Qing Dynasty

3. **What is the admission price to the Forbidden City in May?**

   (A) 40 RMB

   (B) 50 RMB

   (C) 60 RMB

EXERCISE TWO: QUESTIONS

1. **Where is Beihai Park located?**

   (A) East of the Forbidden City

   (B) Downtown Beijing

   (C) Near the North Sea

2. **Why would a visit to Beihai Park be worthwhile?**

   (A) You can learn about Chinese history.

   (B) You can have a meal while taking a cruise.

   (C) You can relax and watch the animals.

3. **Which of the following is NOT supported by the passage?**

   (A) Most visitors to Beihai are foreigners.

   (B) Beihai was expanded during later dynasties.

   (C) Beihai has a history of about one thousand years.

Translation Exercise

NAME _____ COURSE _____ DATE _____

Translate the following sentences into Pinyin romanization with correct tone marks. If you have forgotten a word, consult the English-Chinese Glossary in the back of your textbook.

1. **How long really is the Great Wall?**

2. **There died I don't know how many people.**

3. **Look! We've finally climbed onto the Great Wall!**

4. **Today I finally had a chance to eat Beijing roast duck.**

5. **These last few weeks sure have been cold!** (use **gòu...-de**)

Character Practice Sheet

NAME _____ COURSE _____ DATE _____

底	丶	亠	广	广	庁	庄	底	底		
建	コ	⊐	⇒	⇒	⇒	聿	建	建		
修	丿	亻	彳	仆	佟	修	修	修		
靠	丶	亠	屮	牛	牛	告	告	苎	苎	苎
	靠	靠	靠	靠	靠					
战	卜	卜	卜	占	占	占	战	战	战	
争	丿	𠂉	𠂊	刍	刍	争				

Reading and Writing Exercises

NAME _____ COURSE _____ DATE _____

A. Transcribe what you hear in the online audio into Chinese characters.

(1)

(2)

(3)

B. If a reference is given after a question, answer based on the referenced part of the Reading Exercises. If no reference is indicated, you may answer any way you wish.

(1) 万里长城是什么时候修建的？ A1

(2) 你觉得爱情可靠不可靠？房子是不是比男人更可靠？ A7

(3) 那部电影是哪一类的电影？是关于什么的？ A8

(4) 长城到底有多长？

Emergencies (I)

PART ONE

Listening Comprehension Exercises

NAME _____ COURSE _____ DATE _____

Based on the recorded passages, circle the best response to each of the questions that follow. You may listen to each passage as many times as needed.

EXERCISE ONE: QUESTIONS

1. **What will the student do tomorrow?**

   (A) Go to class

   (B) Stay home

   (C) Go see a doctor

2. **Which of these symptoms DOESN'T the student have?**

   (A) Fever

   (B) Headache

   (C) Weakness

3. **Based on the passage, which of the following descriptions is the most accurate?**

   (A) Classrooms are cold but outside it's warm.

   (B) Outside it's cold but classrooms are warm.

   (C) Classrooms are cold and outside it's also cold.

4. **Which of these suggestions is NOT mentioned in the passage?**

   (A) Wear warm clothes.

   (B) Get enough rest.

   (C) Drink lots of hot water.

EXERCISE TWO: QUESTIONS

1. **When the man's illness began, what was his first symptom?**

   (A) Fever

   (B) Headache

   (C) Nausea

2. **Which of these symptoms does he NOT have?**

   (A) Fever

   (B) Headache

   (C) Nausea

3. **What is the doctor's recommendation about the man's illness?**

   (A) It's going to turn into pneumonia.

   (B) The man needs lots of rest to get better.

   (C) The man needn't worry as his illness isn't serious.

Translation Exercise

NAME _____ COURSE _____ DATE _____

Translate the following sentences into Pinyin romanization with correct tone marks. If you have forgotten a word, consult the English-Chinese Glossary in the back of your textbook.

1. **It seems like I have a bit of fever.**

2. **I don't think I need to go to a hospital.**

3. **He can't speak English very well.** (use **bú dà**)

4. **If you don't feel well, it's best to see a doctor sooner.**

5. **The three of us have headaches, are nauseous, and feel like throwing up.**

Character Practice Sheet

NAME _____ COURSE _____ DATE _____

医	一	丁	〒	匚	医	医	医			
院	㇇	阝	阝'	阝'	阝一	阝二	阵	阹	院	
变	丶	亠	十	亣	亦	亦	变	变		
许	丶	讠	讠'	讠ⸯ	许	许				
志	一	十	士	士	志	志	志			
英	一	十	艹	节	芇	苩	荚	英		

Reading and Writing Exercises

NAME _____ COURSE _____ DATE _____

A. **Transcribe what you hear in the online audio into Chinese characters.**

(1)

(2)

(3)

B. **If a reference is given after a question, answer based on the referenced part of the Reading Exercises. If no reference is indicated, you may answer any way you wish.**

(1) 高英华夫人是不是说过广州过几年一定还有更大的变化？ B1

(2) 许志明同志觉得英国的医生怎么样？英国的医院怎么样？ C1

(3) 你相信气候变化吗？

(4) 离你家最近的电影院叫什么？

PART TWO

Listening Comprehension Exercises

NAME_____ COURSE_____ DATE_____

Based on the recorded passages, circle the best response to each of the questions that follow. You may listen to each passage as many times as needed.

EXERCISE ONE: QUESTIONS

1. **What was stolen?**
   - (A) A backpack
   - (B) A purse
   - (C) A wallet

2. **When did the incident take place?**
   - (A) In the morning
   - (B) In the afternoon
   - (C) In the evening

3. **Where did the incident take place?**
   - (A) A restaurant
   - (B) A supermarket
   - (C) On the street

EXERCISE TWO: QUESTIONS

1. **Where was the wallet probably stolen?**
   - (A) Bank
   - (B) Post office
   - (C) Supermarket

2. **What was in the wallet?**
   - (A) Passport
   - (B) Library card
   - (C) Identification papers

3. **What is the man advised to do now?**
   - (A) Call a policeman
   - (B) Look for the wallet
   - (C) Inform authorities

Translation Exercise

NAME _____ COURSE _____ DATE _____

Translate the following sentences into Pinyin romanization with correct tone marks. If you have forgotten a word, consult the English-Chinese Glossary in the back of your textbook.

1. **He was scolded by his mother.**

2. **Thief! Someone stole my wallet!**

3. **I must get my purse back!** (use **fēi...bù kě**)

4. **A: What happened? B: We were deceived!**

5. **Don't get excited; we'll definitely do our best to help you.**

Character Practice Sheet

NAME _____ COURSE _____ DATE _____

偷	′	⺅	⺅	价	价	价	价	偷	偷	偷
	偷									
赶	一	十	土	走	走	走	走	走	走	赶
读	′	讠	讠	讠	读	读	读	读	读	读
护	一	扌	扌	护	护	护	护			
皮	⺂	厂	广	皮	皮					
被	′	衤	衤	衤	衤	衤	衤	被	被	被

Reading and Writing Exercises

NAME _____ COURSE _____ DATE _____

A. Transcribe what you hear in the online audio into Chinese characters.

(1)

(2)

(3)

B. If a reference is given after a question, answer based on the referenced part of the Reading Exercises. If no reference is indicated, you may answer any way you wish.

(1) 他们为什么得快一点儿赶到车站？ A8

(2) 王大海有什么问题？ A10

(3) 你有几双皮鞋？

(4) 你每天读几个小时书？

Emergencies (II)

PART ONE

Listening Comprehension Exercises

NAME _____ COURSE _____ DATE _____

Based on the recorded passages, circle the best response to each of the questions that follow. You may listen to each passage as many times as needed.

EXERCISE ONE: QUESTIONS

1. **What is the topic of the passage?**

   (A) A stolen purse

   (B) A lost bag

   (C) A lost wallet

2. **What is the best description of the missing item?**

   (A) Green and black

   (B) Black and red

   (C) Black and yellow

3. **What was NOT in the missing item?**

   (A) Books

   (B) Pens

   (C) Wallet

EXERCISE TWO: QUESTIONS

1. **Where is the female speaker's library card?**

   (A) It was stolen.

   (B) She can't find it.

   (C) She lent it to someone else.

2. **When should she return the library card to the man?**

   (A) By this afternoon

   (B) By tomorrow

   (C) By next Monday

3. **What is the maximum number of books that can be borrowed at one time?**

   (A) Five books

   (B) Eight books

   (C) Ten books

Translation Exercise

NAME _____ COURSE _____ DATE _____

Translate the following sentences into Pinyin romanization with correct tone marks. If you have forgotten a word, consult the English-Chinese Glossary in the back of your textbook.

1. Your purse is twice as big as mine!

2. Could I borrow a pencil from you?

3. Yesterday I lost my student I.D.; I wonder if anybody found it?

4. When you're finished using these things, please give them back to me.

5. I have a very big book bag; on it, there is written "New York Yankees."

Character Practice Sheet

NAME _____ COURSE _____ DATE _____

掉	一	十	扌	扩	扩	扩	护	捗	掉
	掉								
火	丶	丷	少	火					
检	一	十	才	木	朴	朴	柊	柊	检
	检								
查	一	十	木	木	术	杏	杳	査	查
危	丿	𠂊	产	产	危	危			
险	了	阝	阝	阶	险	险	险	险	

Reading and Writing Exercises

NAME _____ COURSE _____ DATE _____

A. **Transcribe what you hear in the online audio into Chinese characters.**

(1)

(2)

(3)

B. **If a reference is given after a question, answer based on the referenced part of the Reading Exercises. If no reference is indicated, you may answer any way you wish.**

(1) 那个地方为什么很危险？ A6

(2) 那个人要检查什么？为什么？ A8

(3) 你觉得，完全忘掉自己的"根"有没有关系？ C2

(4) 你喜欢坐火车还是坐飞机？

PART TWO

Listening Comprehension Exercises

NAME _____ COURSE _____ DATE _____

Based on the recorded passages, circle the best response to each of the questions that follow. You may listen to each passage as many times as needed.

EXERCISE ONE: QUESTIONS

1. **What type of vehicle hit the bicyclist?**

    (A) Bus

    (B) Car

    (C) Taxi

2. **What happened as a result of the accident?**

    (A) The bicyclist was injured.

    (B) The bicyclist's shirt was torn.

    (C) The bicyclist's bicycle was damaged.

3. **Why did the bicyclist not call the police?**

    (A) The accident was partially his fault.

    (B) The other person was opposed to doing this.

    (C) The bicyclist was afraid of getting into trouble.

4. **In the end, how was this accident resolved?**

    (A) The bicyclist and driver went to the police station.

    (B) The bicyclist and driver each went on his way.

    (C) The driver paid the bicyclist some money.

EXERCISE TWO: QUESTIONS

1. **What item belonging to the speaker was stolen this morning?**

    (A) Cell phone

    (B) Identification

    (C) Passport

2. **When was the speaker hit by a car?**

    (A) On her way home

    (B) On her way to the police station

    (C) On her way to the supermarket

3. **Why was the speaker hit by a car?**

    (A) The speaker wasn't paying attention.

    (B) The car wasn't paying attention to the traffic light.

    (C) The car tried to dodge a bicyclist and ended up hitting the speaker.

4. **How did the speaker get home eventually?**

    (A) By bus

    (B) By taxi

    (C) On foot

Translation Exercise

NAME _____ COURSE _____ DATE _____

Translate the following sentences into Pinyin romanization with correct tone marks. If you have forgotten a word, consult the English-Chinese Glossary in the back of your textbook.

1. **How is she? Was she injured?**

2. **Look, a big hole got torn in my shirt!**

3. **I told him to be careful; as a result, she still had an accident.**

4. **If you do it that way, it's very much not worthwhile.** (use **guài...-de**)

5. **A: He has no money. B: Then we'll just lend him some money and that's it.** (use **déle**)

Character Practice Sheet

NAME _____   COURSE _____   DATE _____

伤	ノ	イ	亻	仵	仿	伤			
破	一	ア	不	石	石	矼	矿	矿	砐	破
结	く	纟	纟	纟	纴	纴	绀	结	结	
发	一	ナ	方	发	发				
费	フ	ヲ	弓	弗	弗	弗	弗	费	费	
合	ノ	人	仝	仐	合	合			

Reading and Writing Exercises

NAME _____ COURSE _____ DATE _____

A. **Transcribe what you hear in the online audio into Chinese characters.**

(1)

(2)

(3)

B. **If a reference is given after a question, answer based on the referenced part of the Reading Exercises. If no reference is indicated, you may answer any way you wish.**

(1) 她考试的结果怎么样？A4

(2) 为什么住校外不太合算？A9

(3) 1850年左右，美国加州发现了什么？C3

(4) 你说中国话，是不是很注意发音？